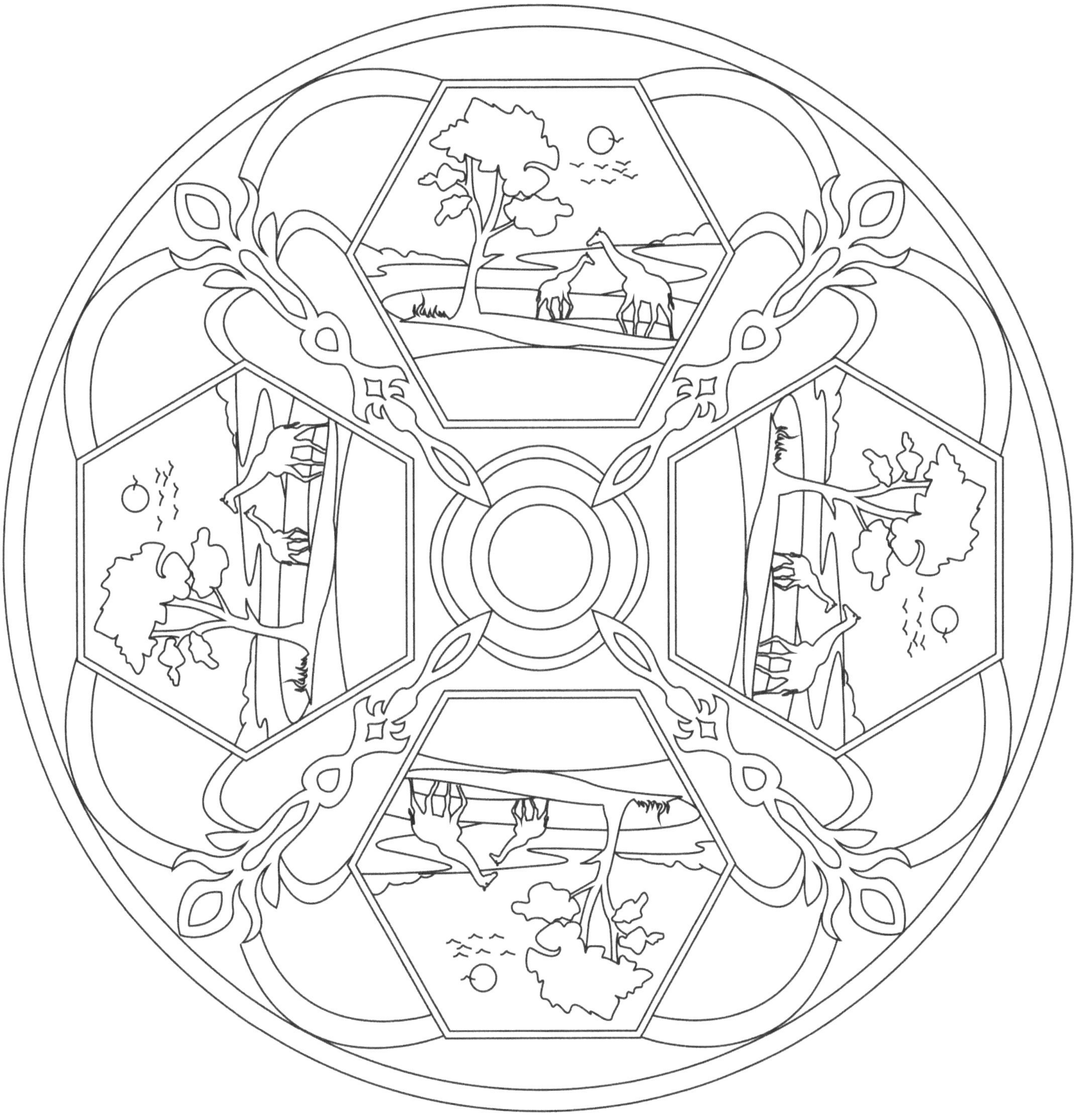

All art is but imitation of nature.

(Lucius Annaeus Seneca)

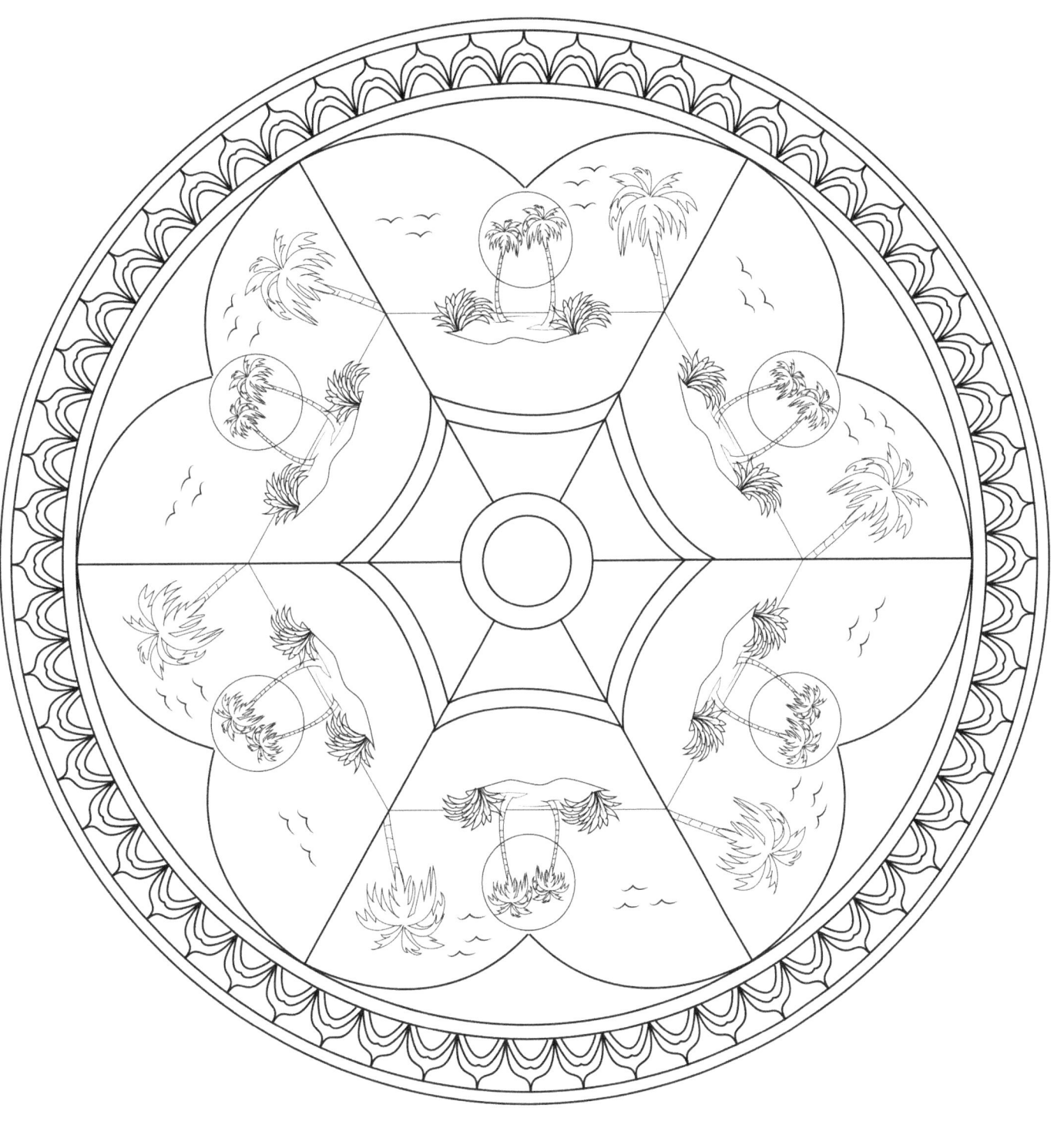

Happiness is not something readymade. It comes from your own actions.

(Dalai Lama)

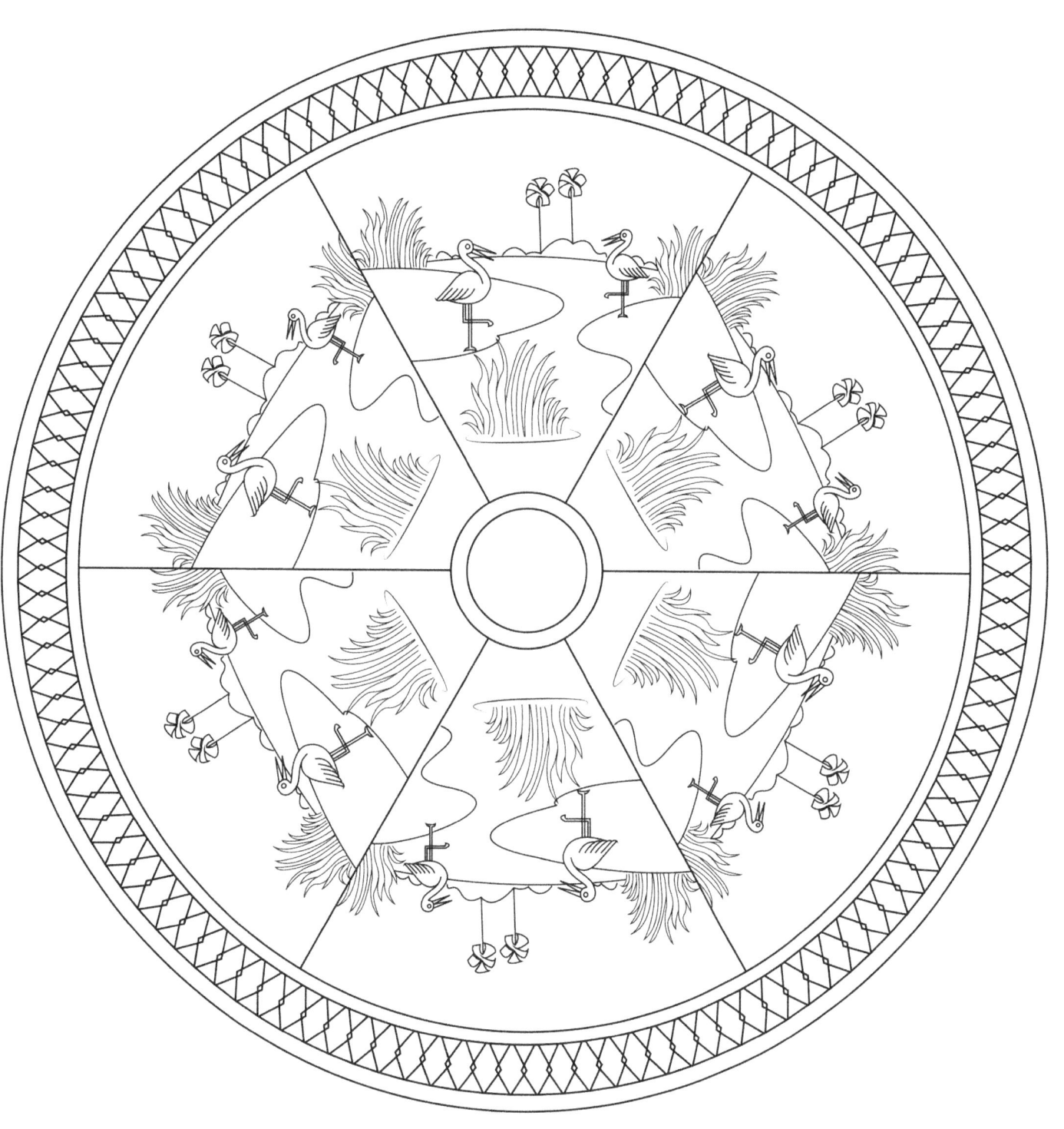

5

Concentration is the secret of strength.

(Franklin Delano Roosevelt)

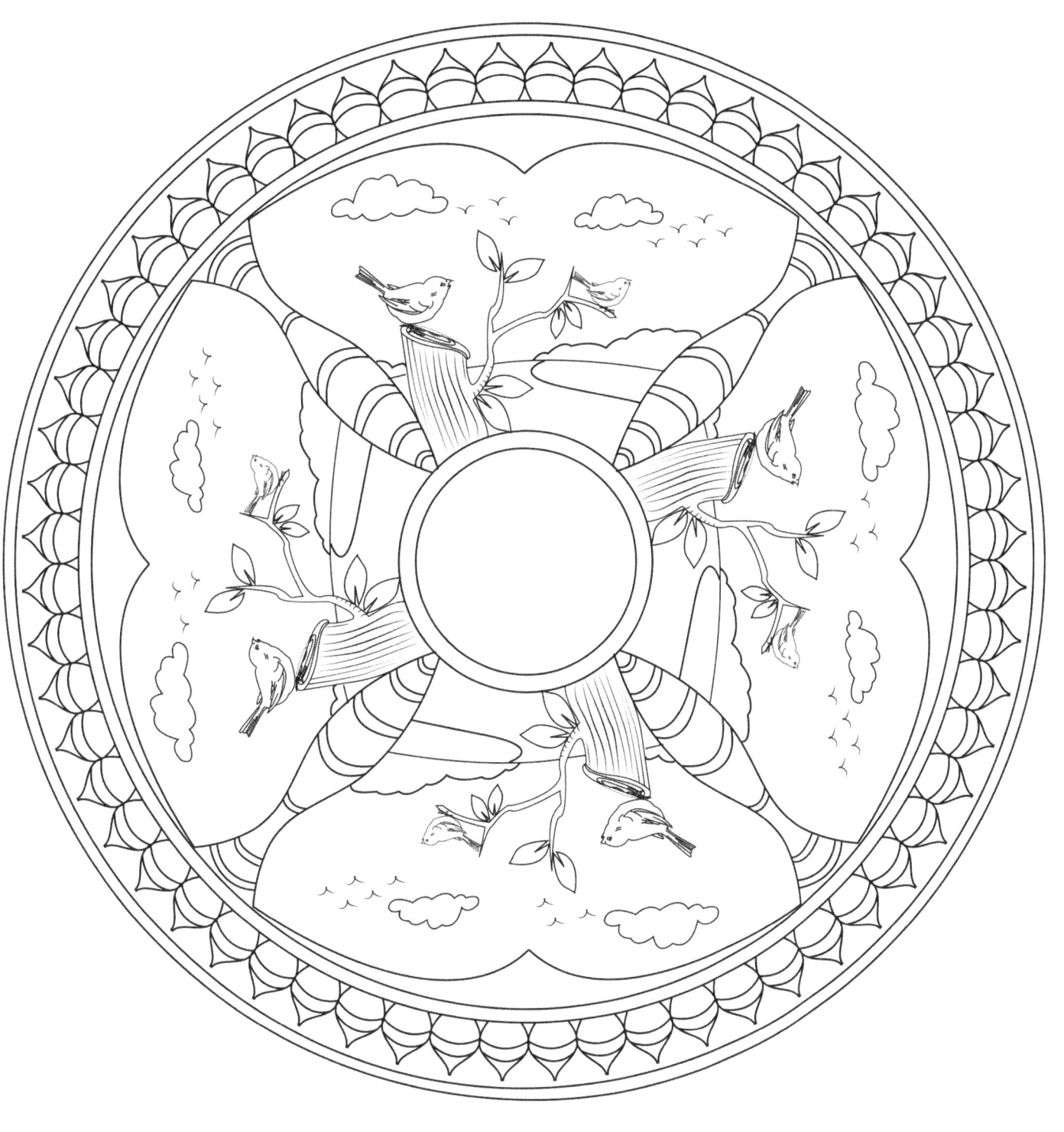

If you want
to find God,
hang out in
the space
between your
thoughts.

(Alan Cohen)

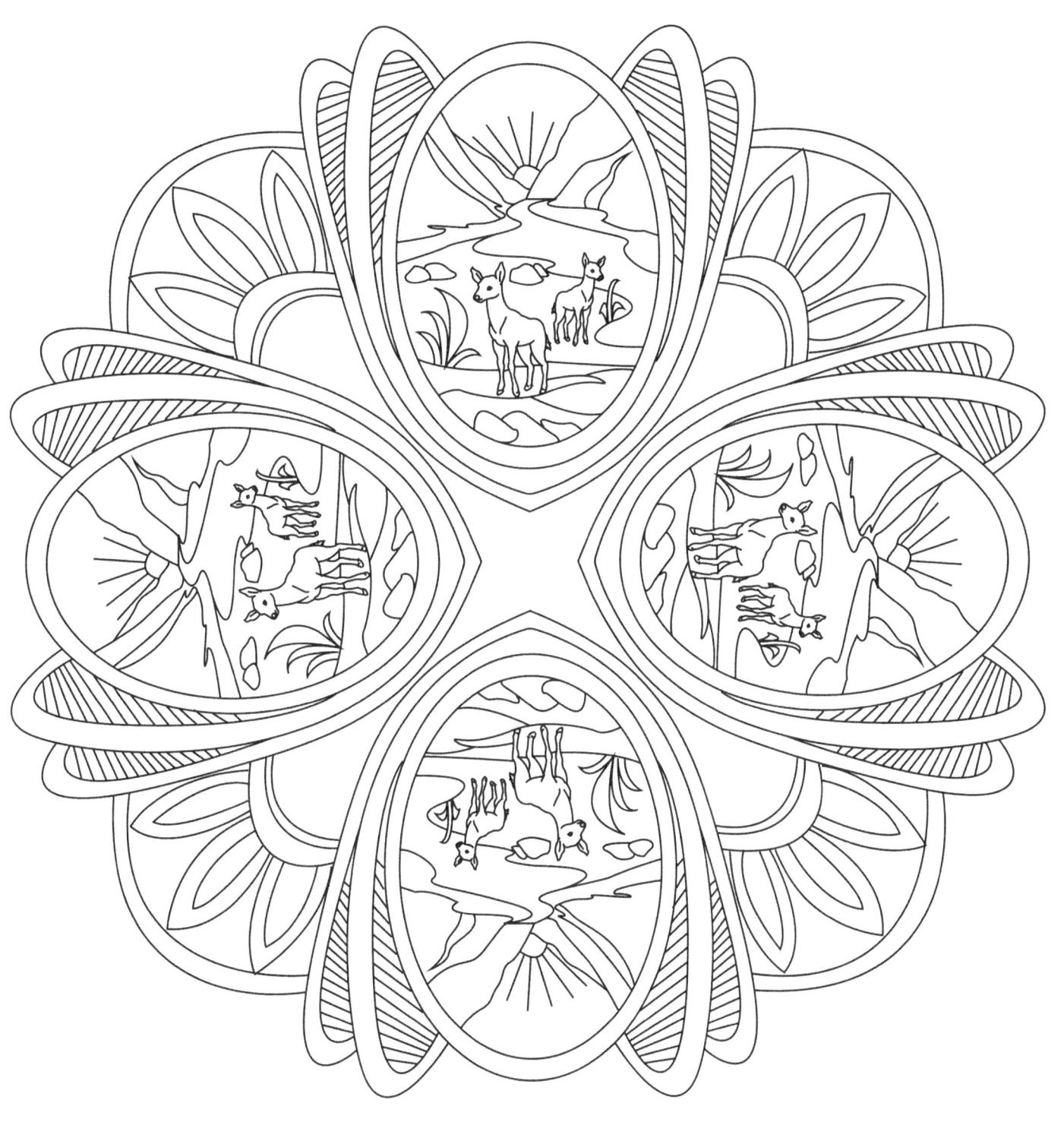

Nature holds the key to our aesthetic, intellectual, cognitive and even spiritual satisfaction.

(E. O. Wilson)

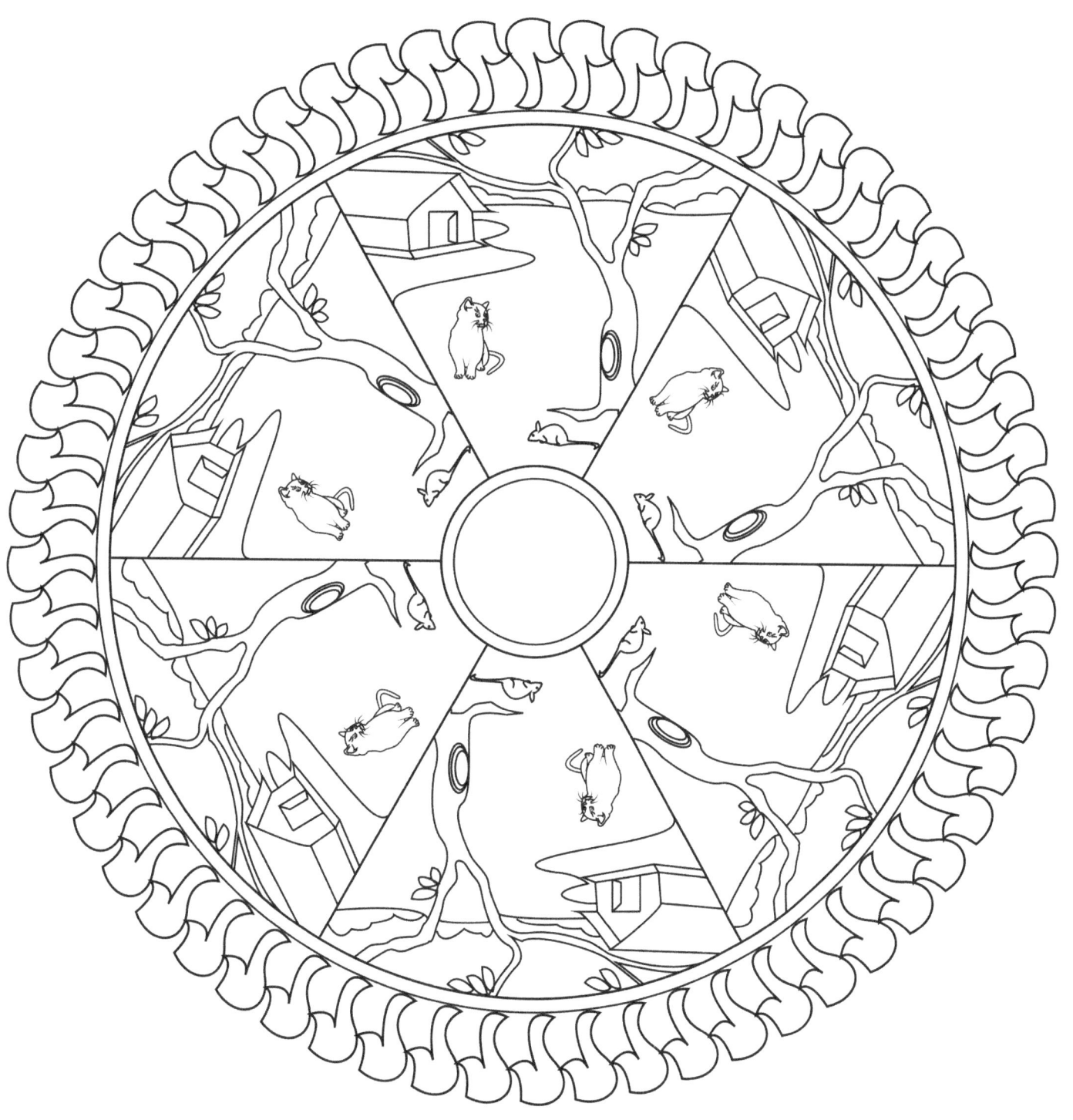

11

The purpose
of art is
washing the
dust of daily
life off our
souls.

(Pablo Picasso)

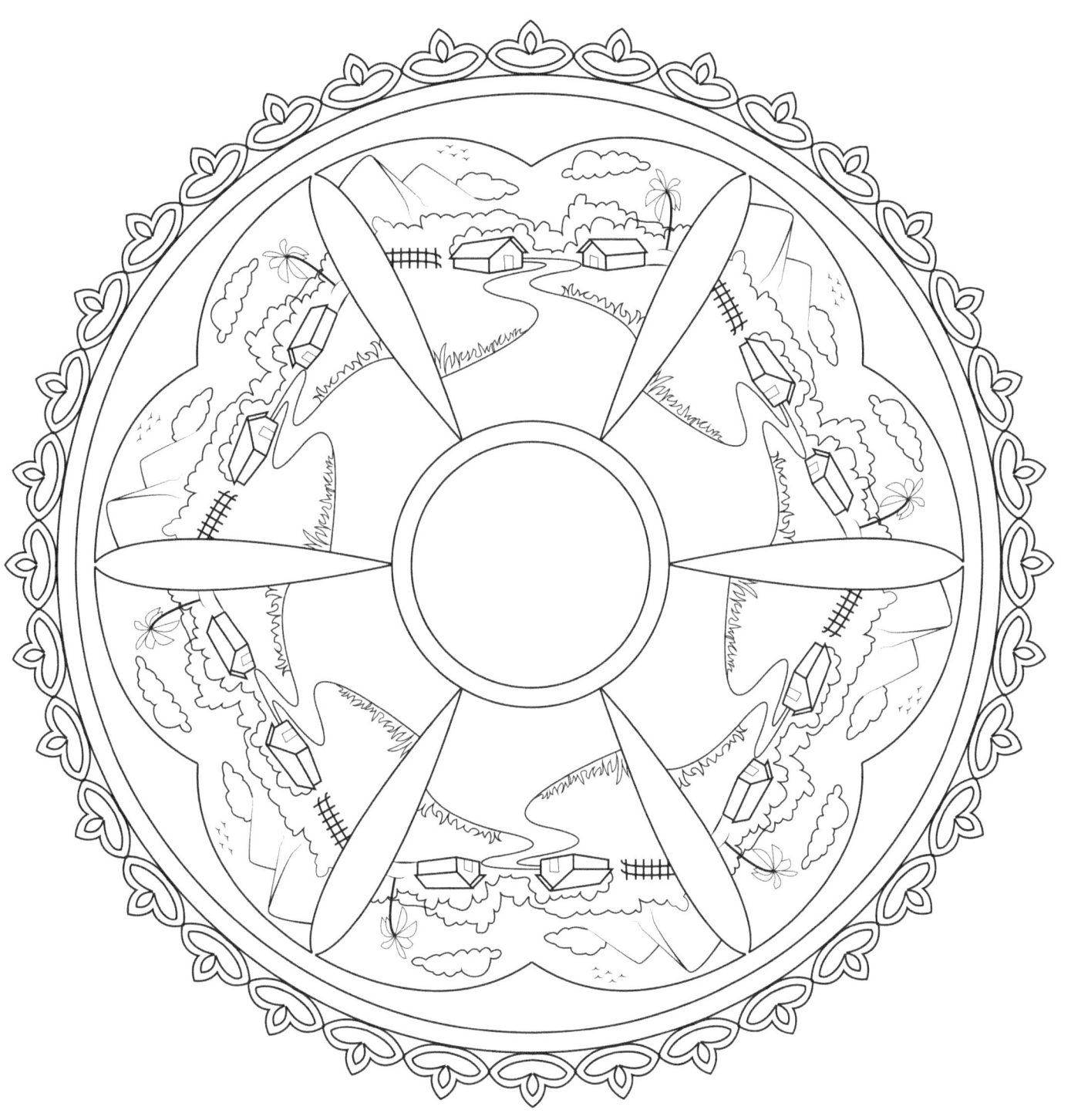

When
I let go of
what I am,
I become
what
I might be.

(Lao Tzu)

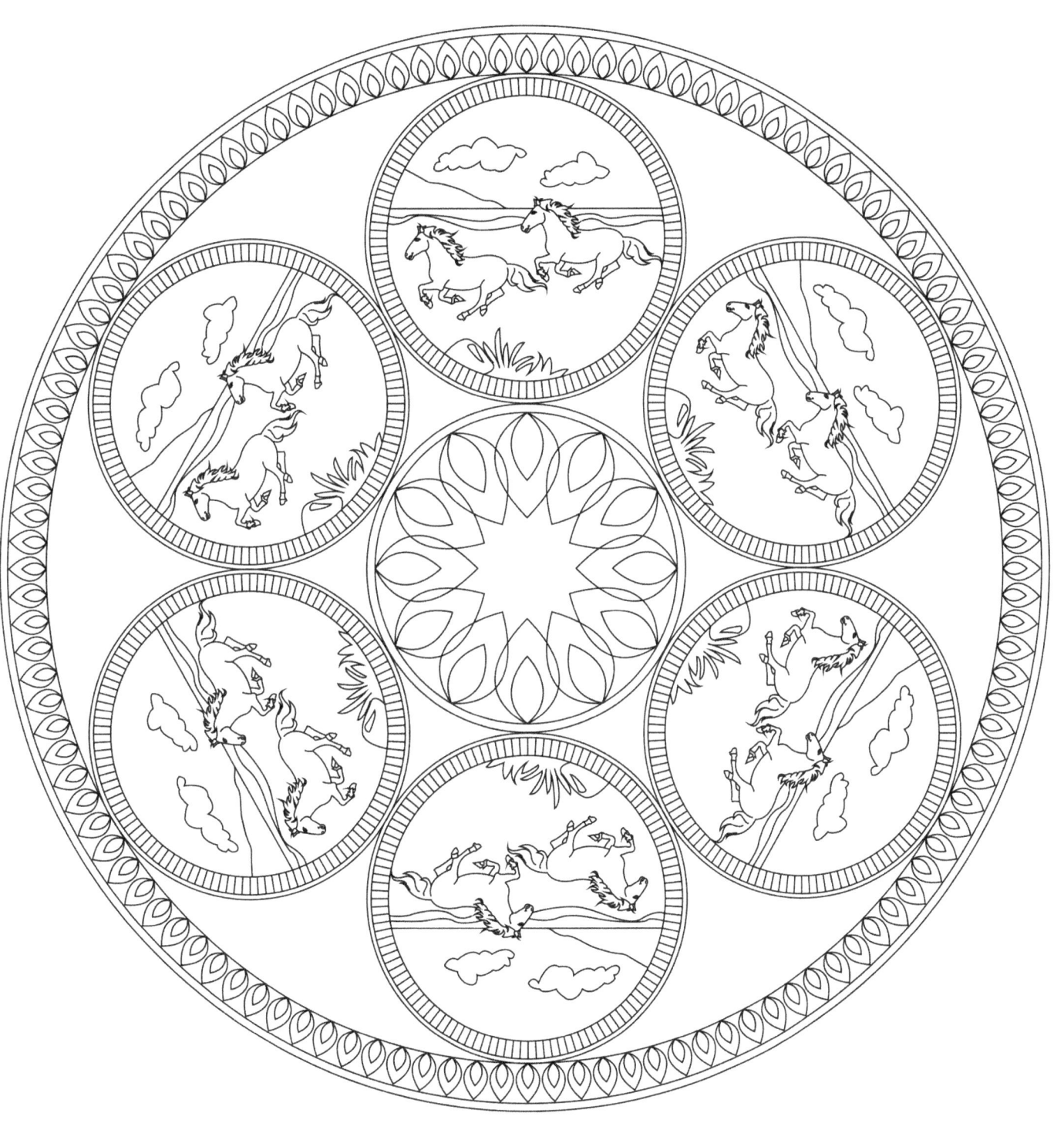

15

Everything
you've ever
wanted
is on the
other side
of fear.

(George Addair)

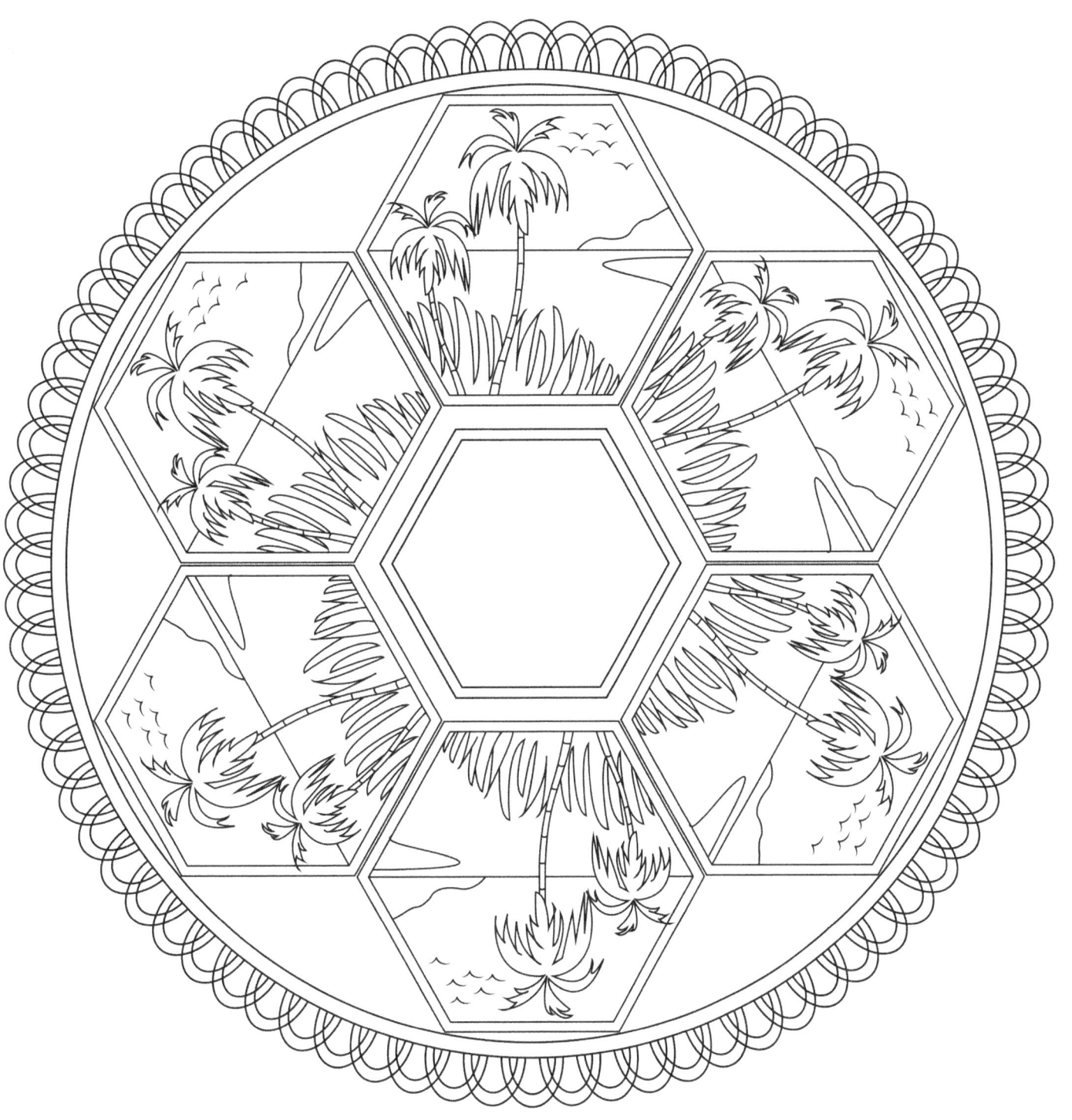

Prayer is
when you
talk to God;
meditation
is when you
listen to
God.

(Diana Robinson)

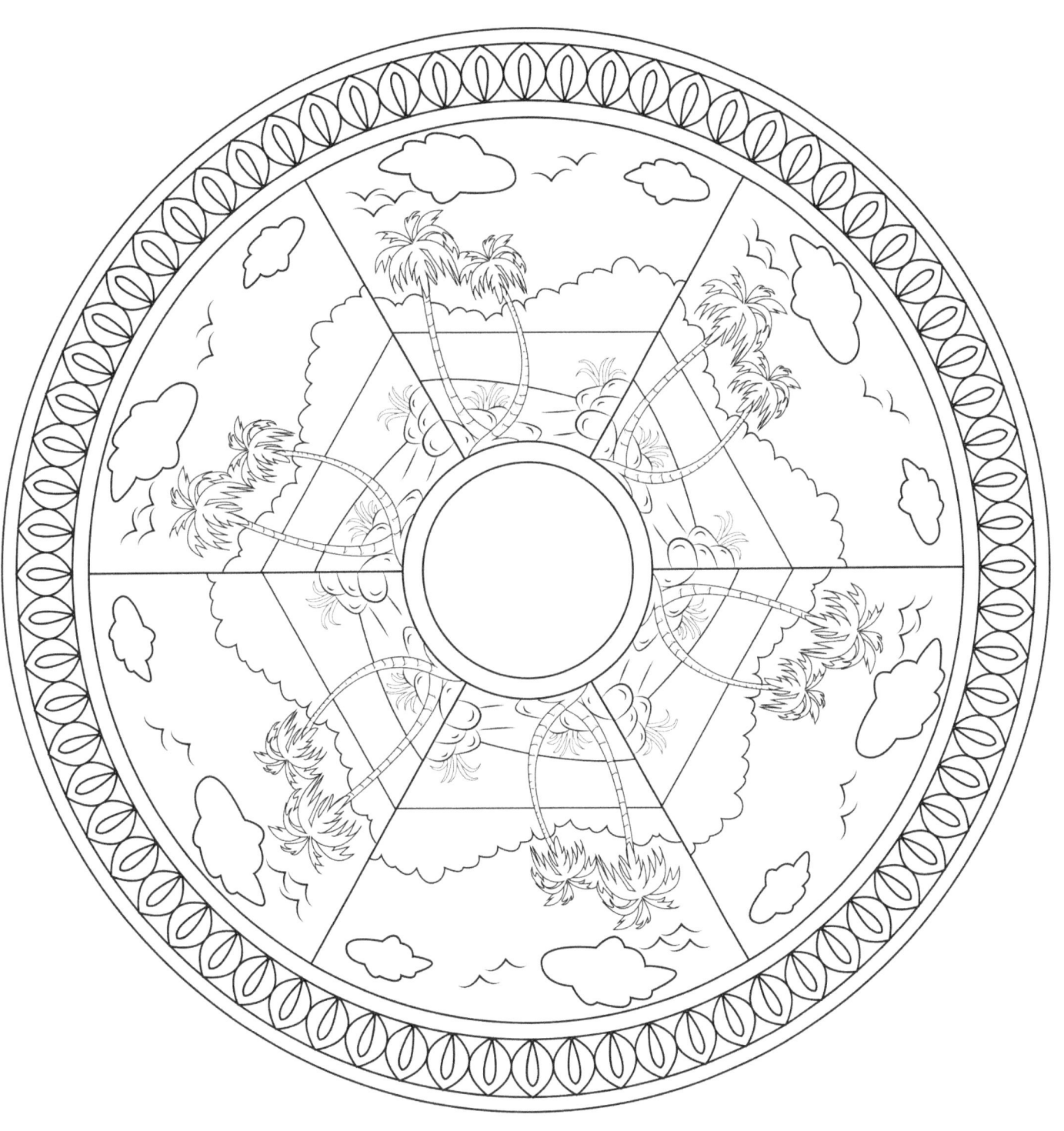

19

The secret of getting ahead is getting started.

(Mark Twain)

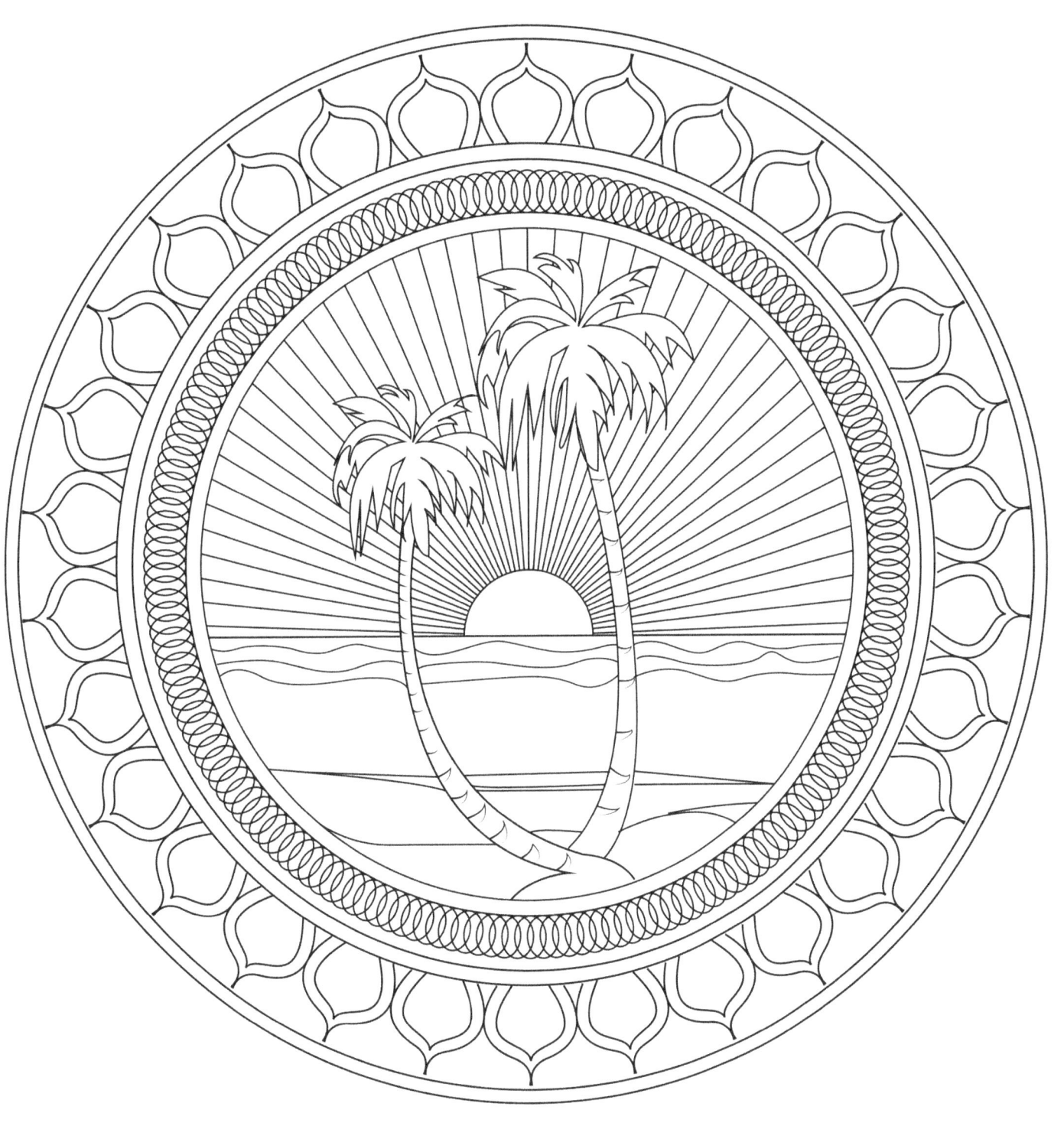

21

If you can
dream it,
you can
do it.

(Walt Disney)

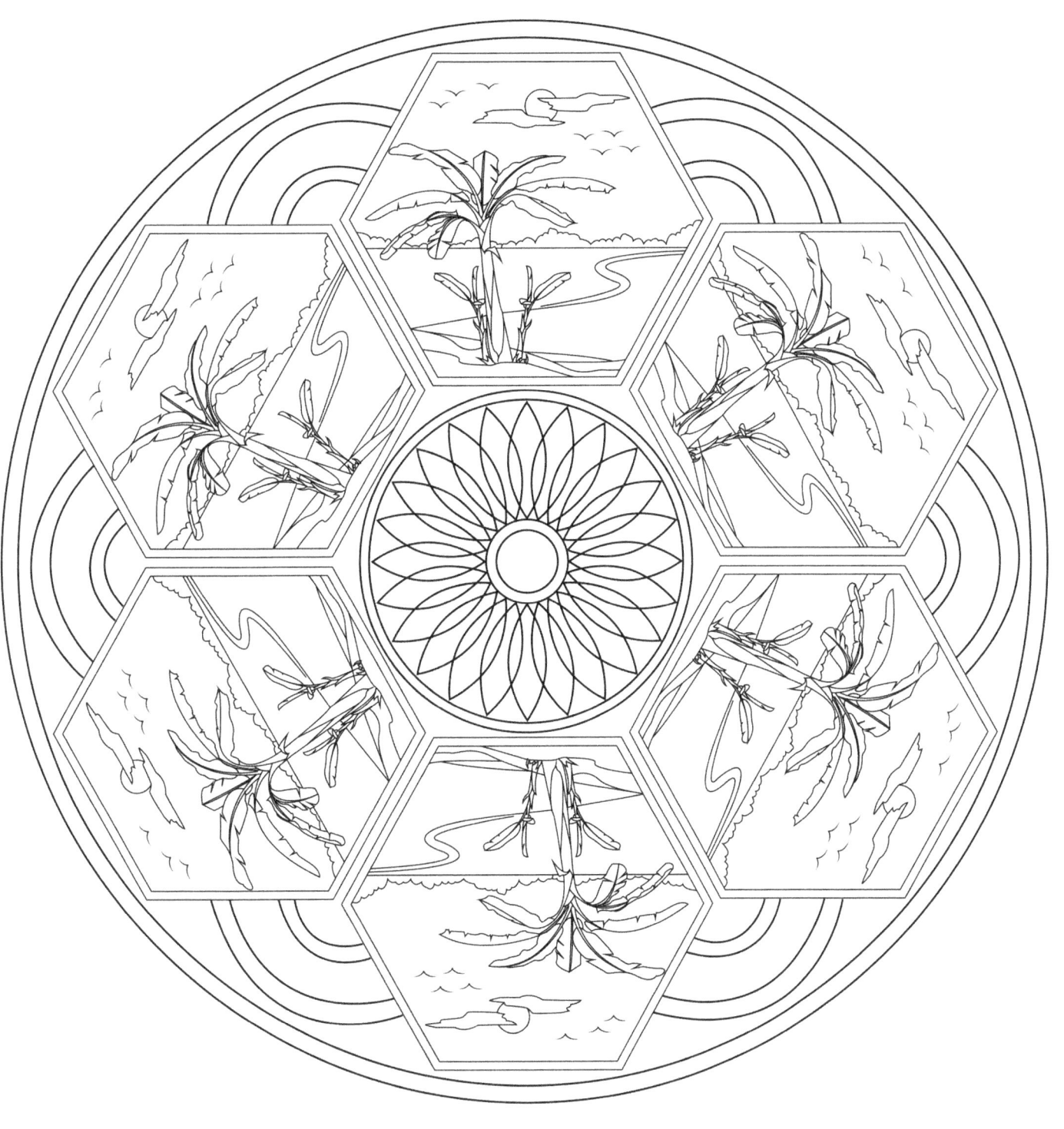

Your calm
mind is the
ultimate
weapon
against your
challenges.
So relax.

(Bryant McGill)

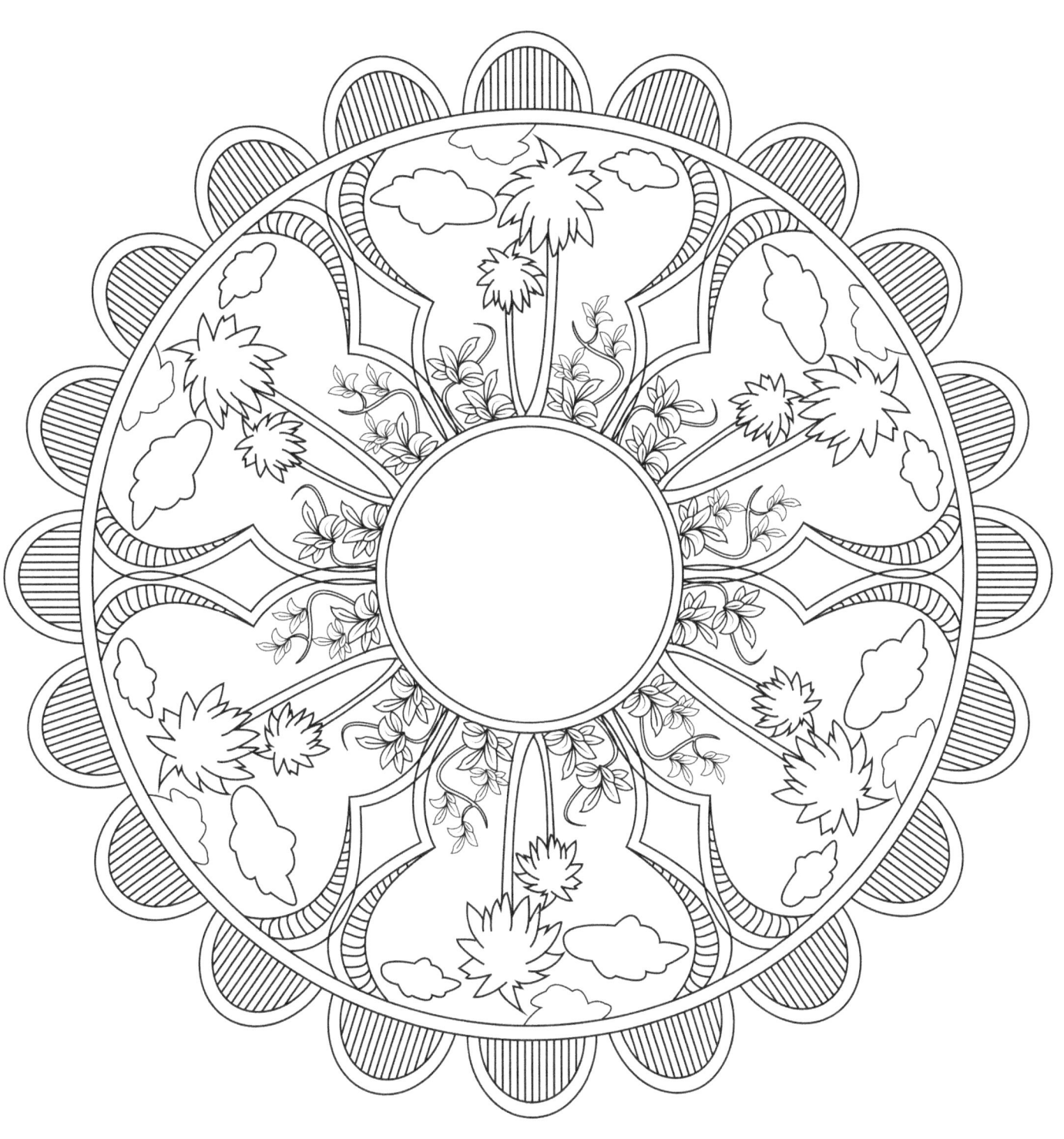

The true meaning of life is to plant trees under whose shade you do not expect to sit.

(Nelson Henderson)

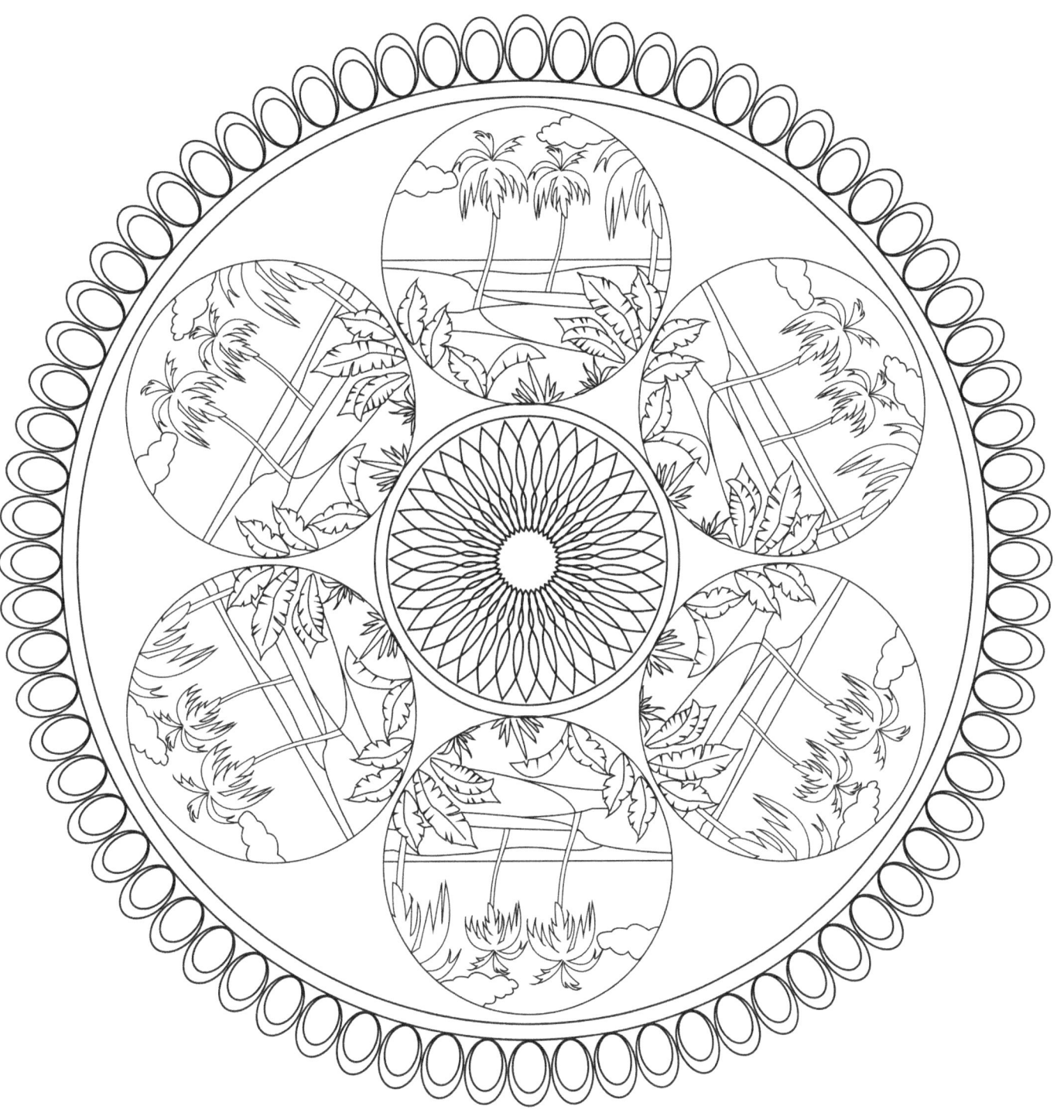

Your talent
is God's gift
to you.
What you
do with it
is your gift
back to God.

(Leo Buscaglia)

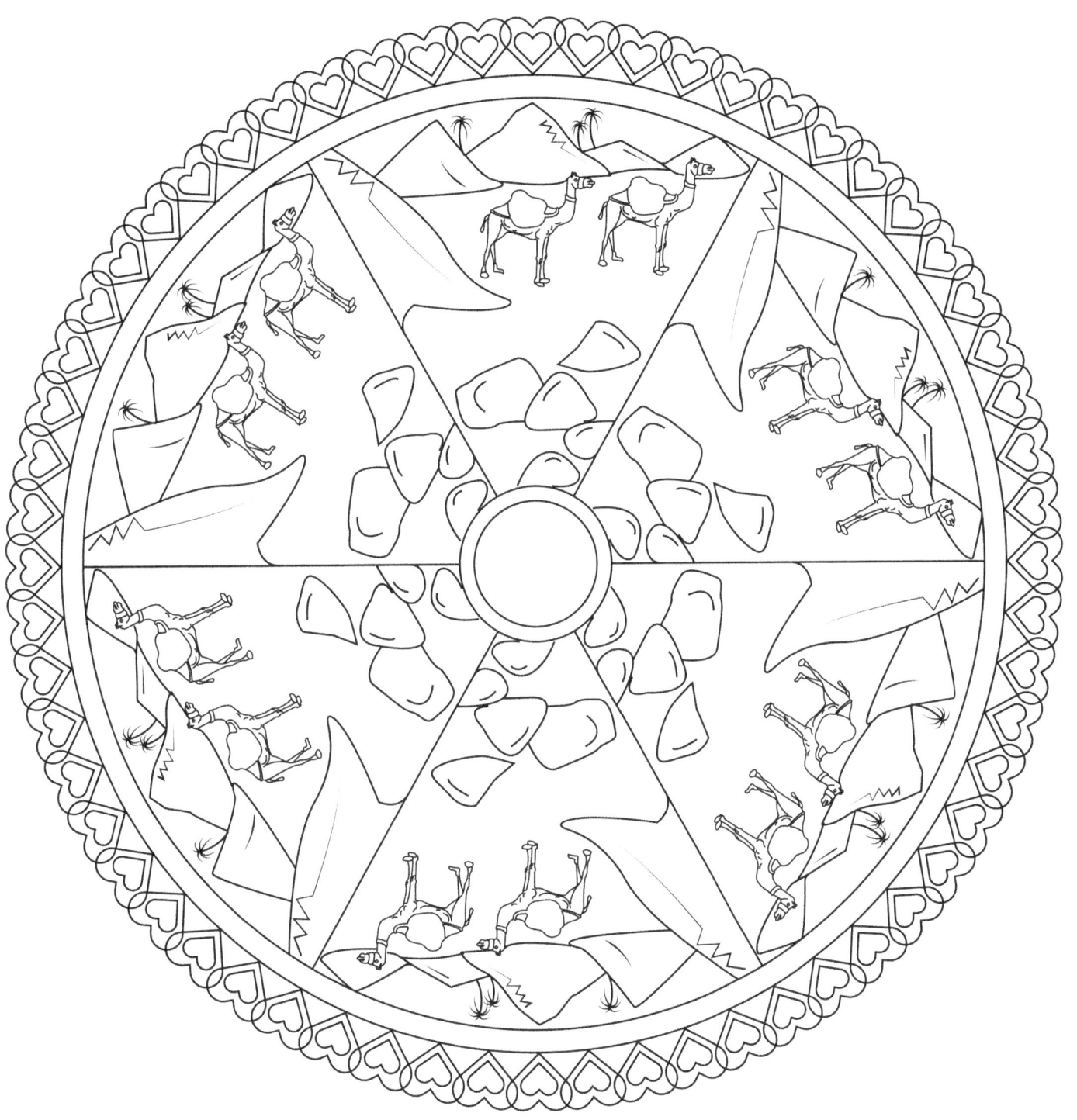

29

Meditation
is not a
means to
an end.
It is both
the means
and the end.

(Jiddu Krishnamurti)

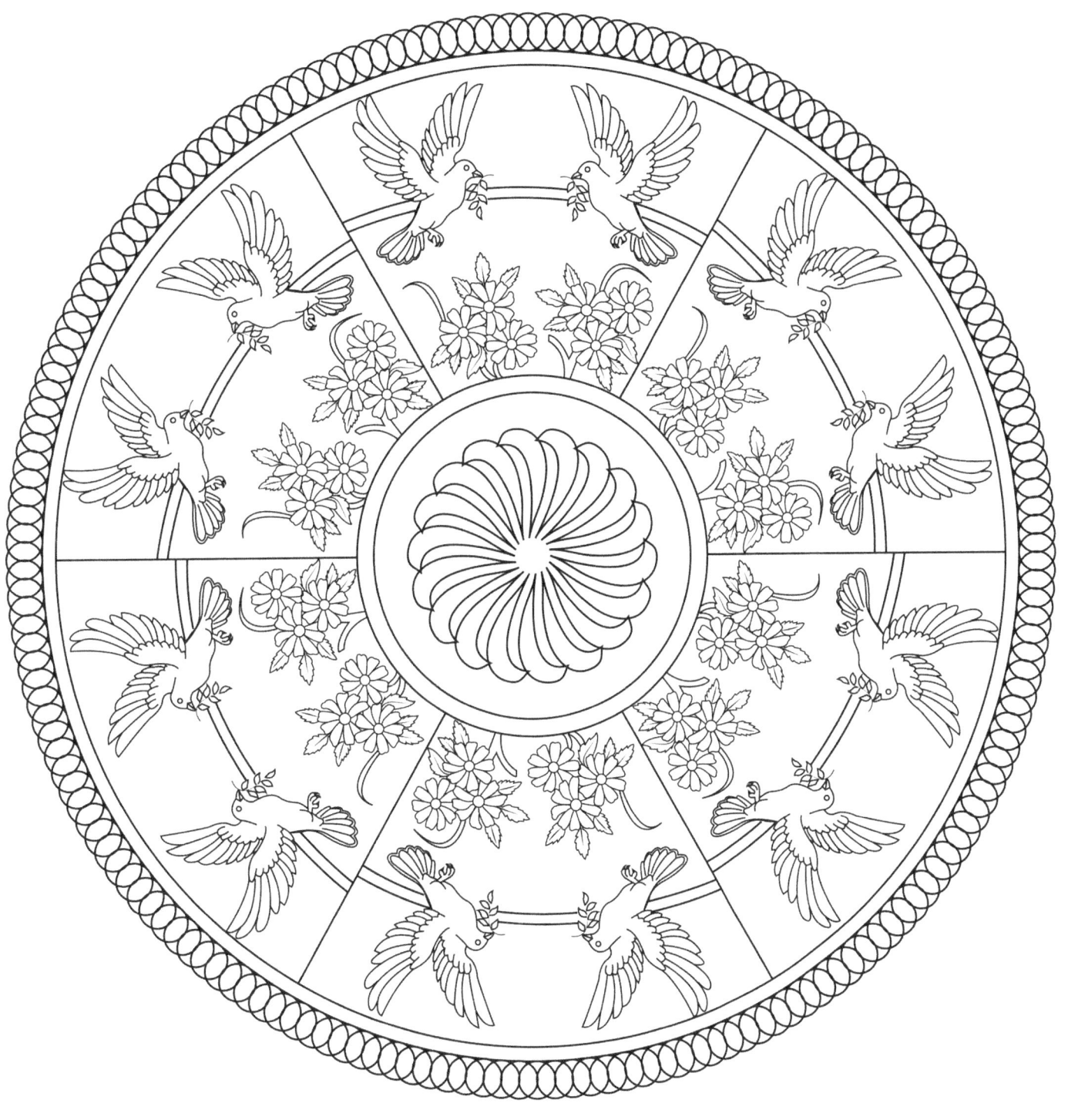

31

Art is like
a border
of flowers
along the
course of
civilization.

(Lincoln Steffens)

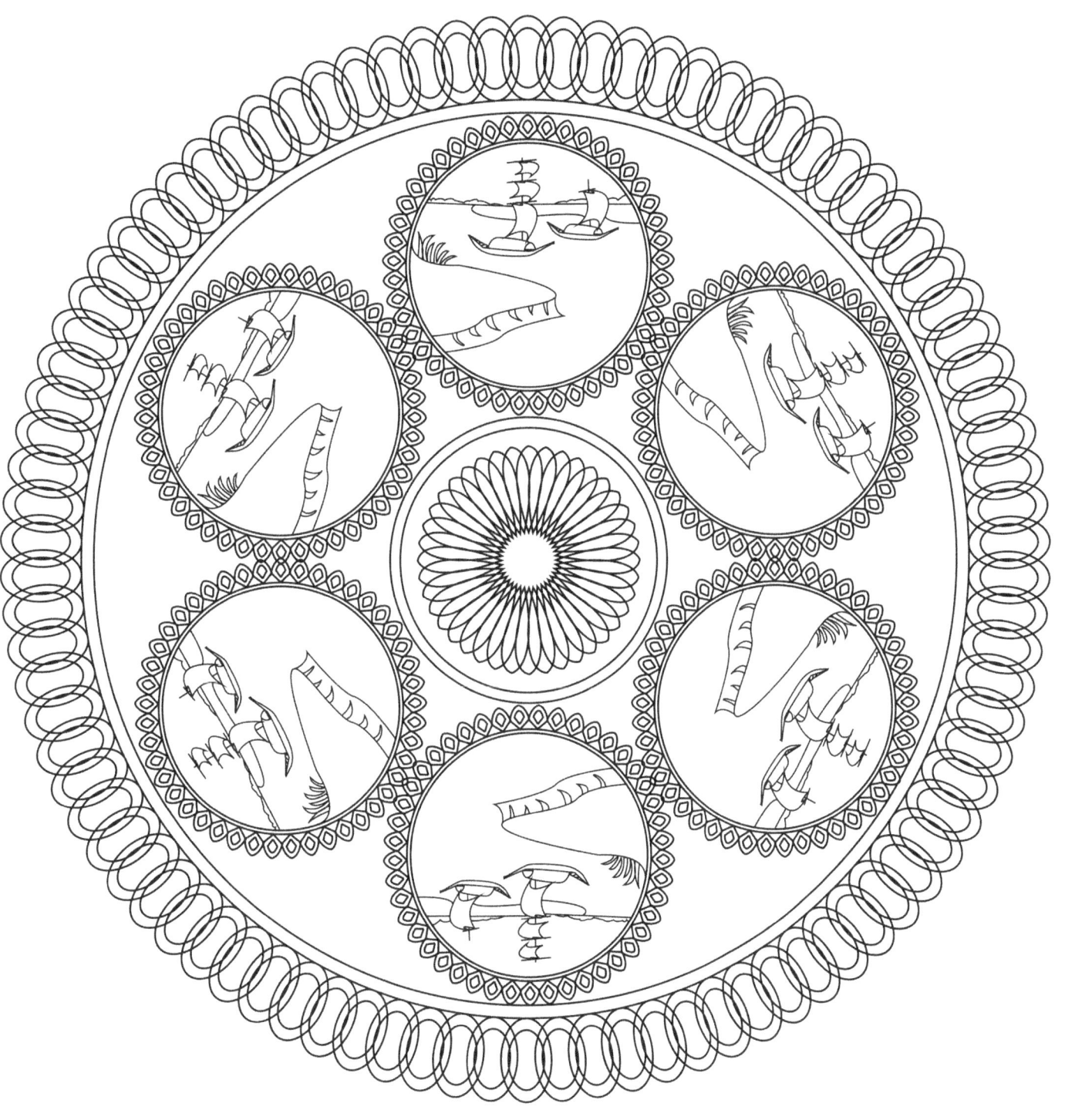

The nature of love is as the nature of water in the depth of the earth. If we do not dig deep enough, we find mud, not water; but when we dig deep, we find pure water.

(Hazrat Inayat Khan)

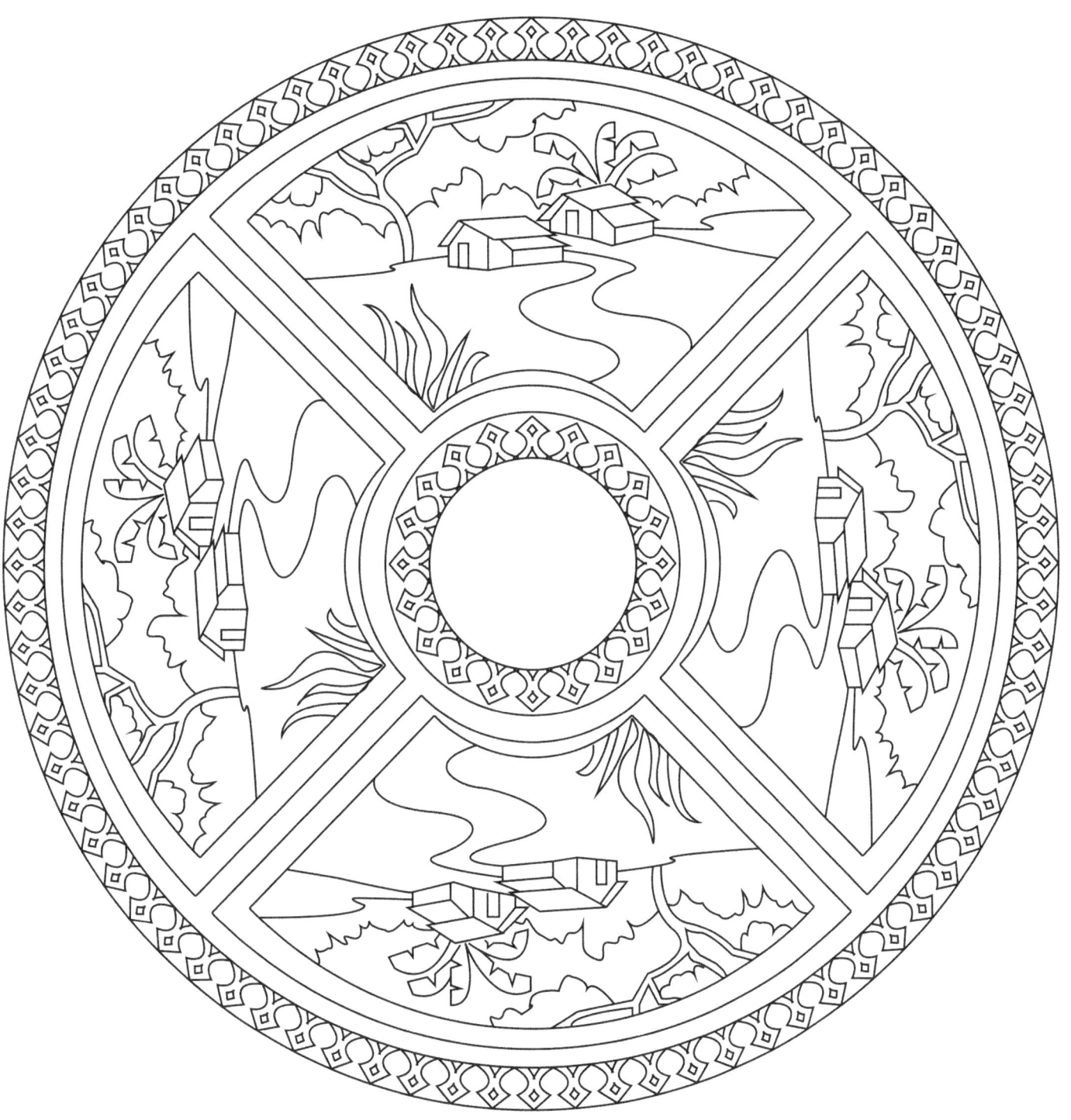

Don't be
pushed
by your
problems.
Be led
by your
dreams.

(Ralph Waldo Emerson)

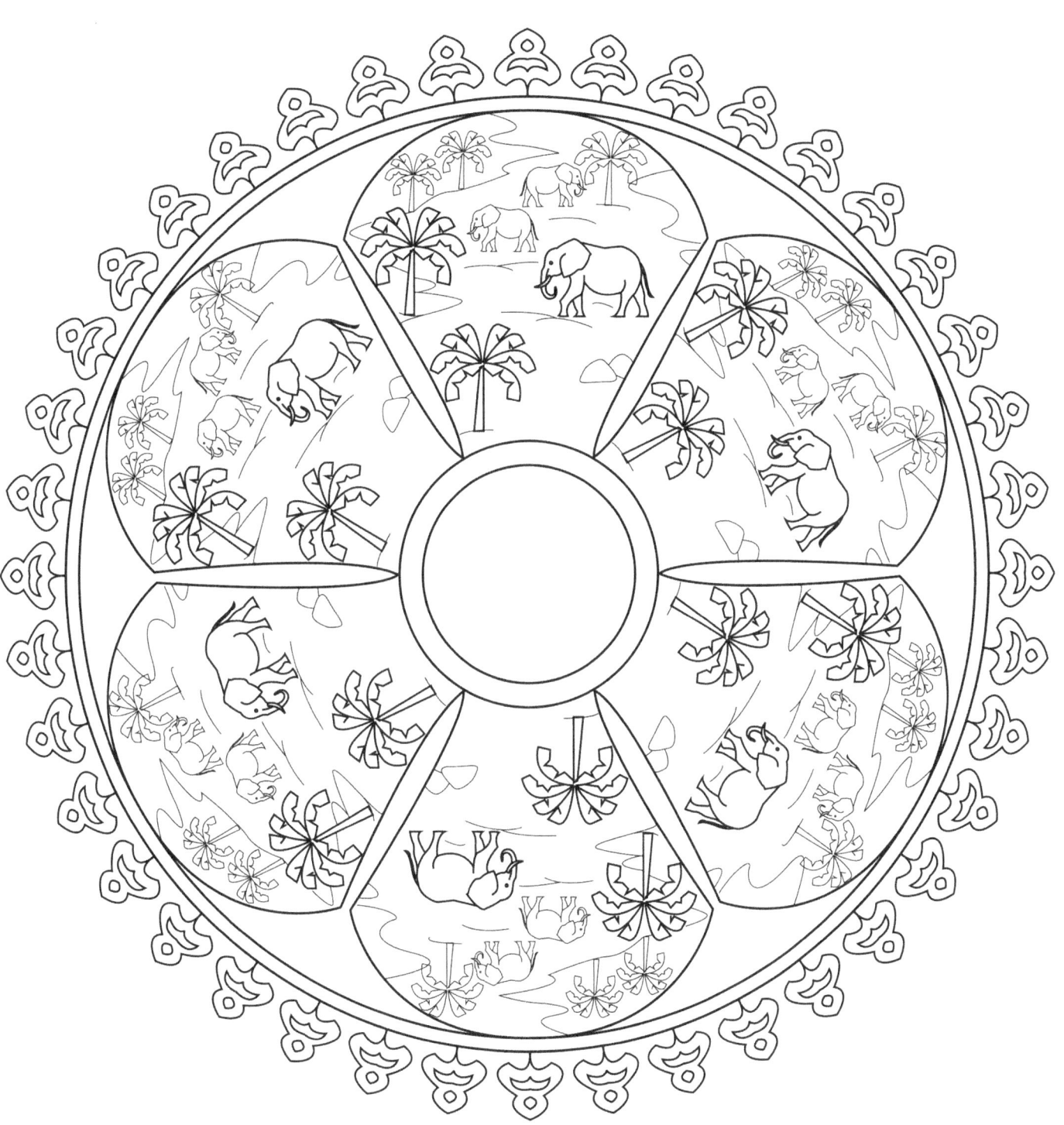

I can
find God
in nature,
in animals,
in birds
and the
environment.

(Pat Buckley)

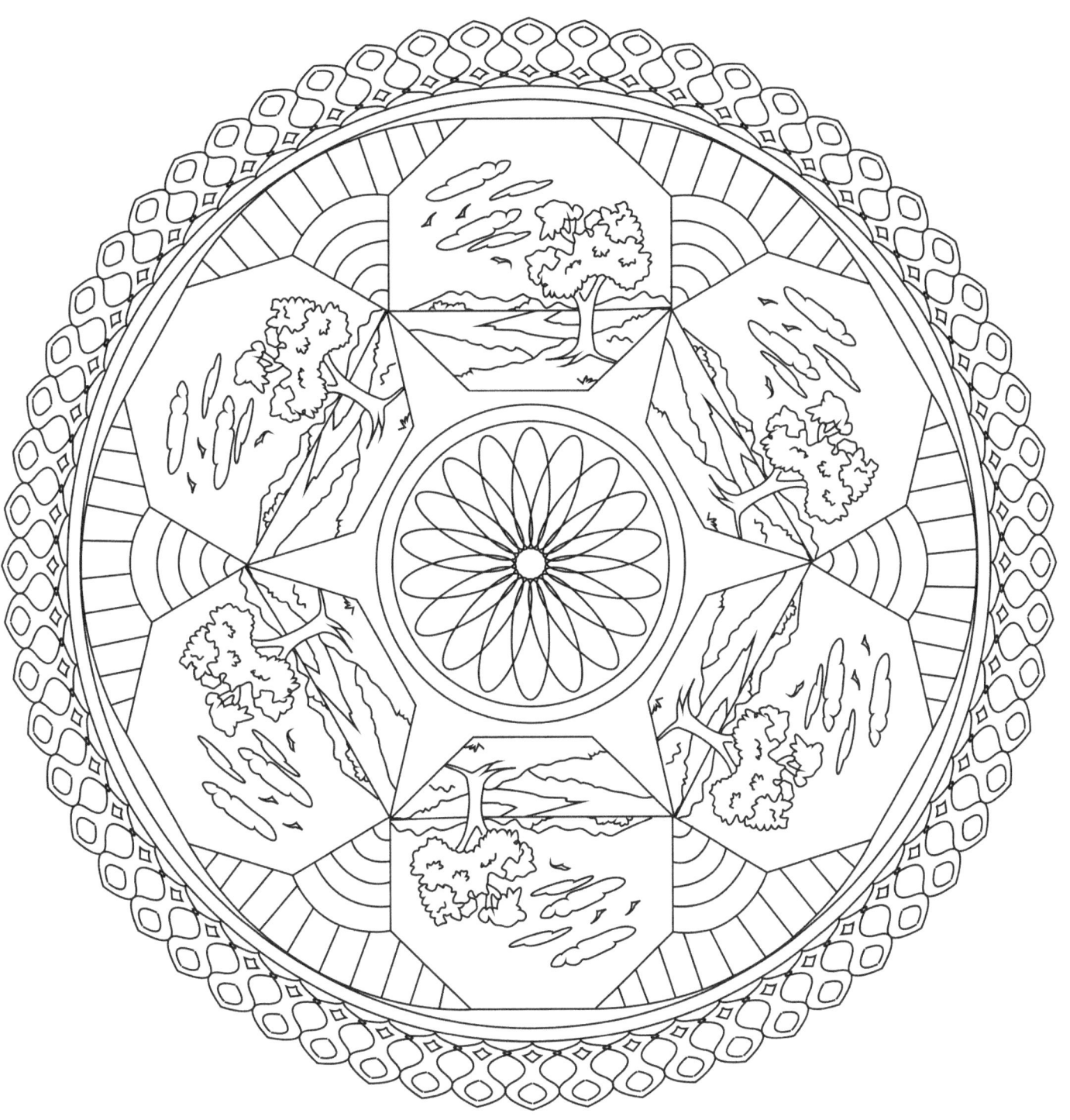

Your
imagination
is your
preview
of life's
coming
attractions.

(Albert Einstein)

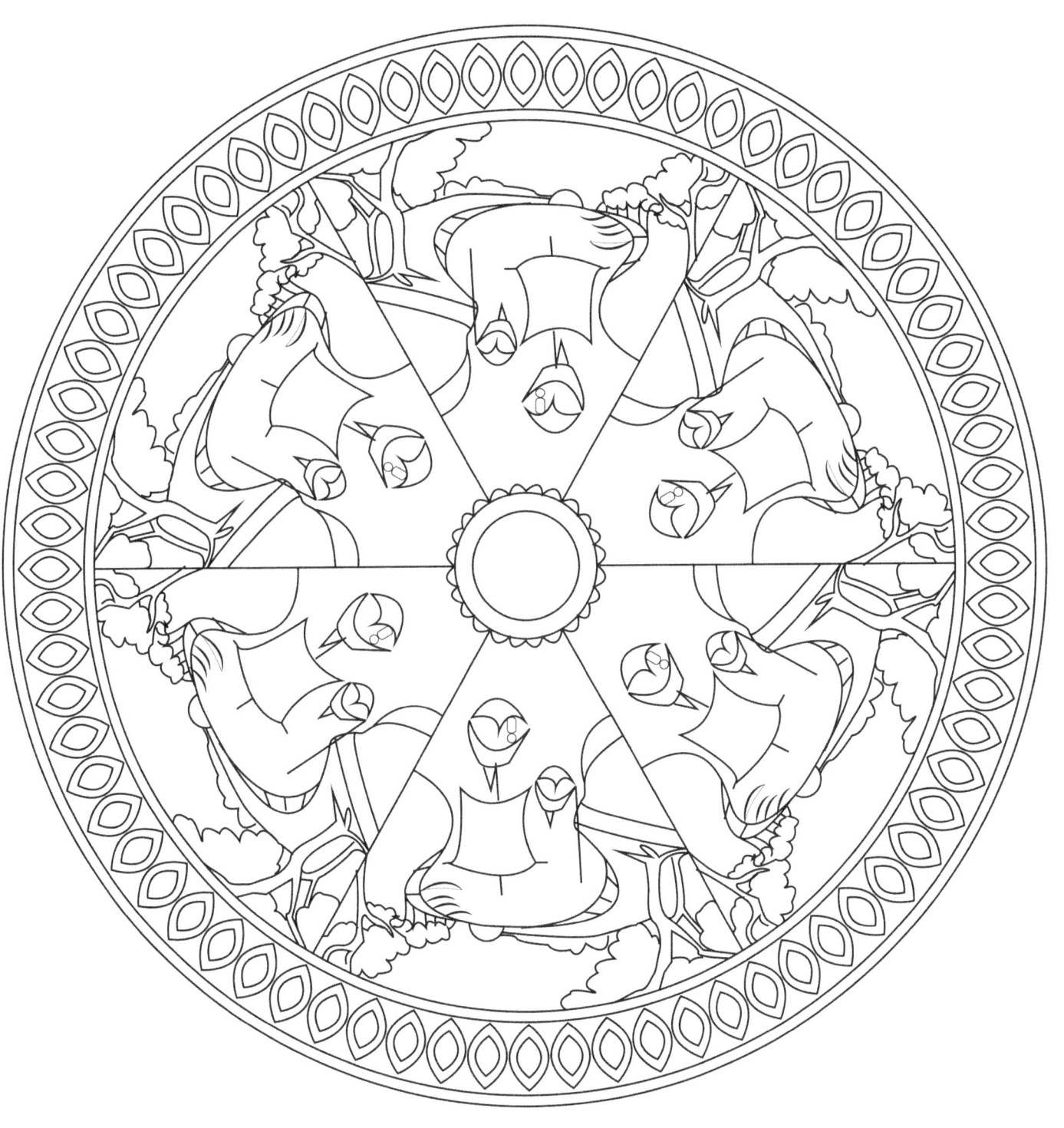

41

We live
in a rainbow
of chaos.

(Paul Cezanne)

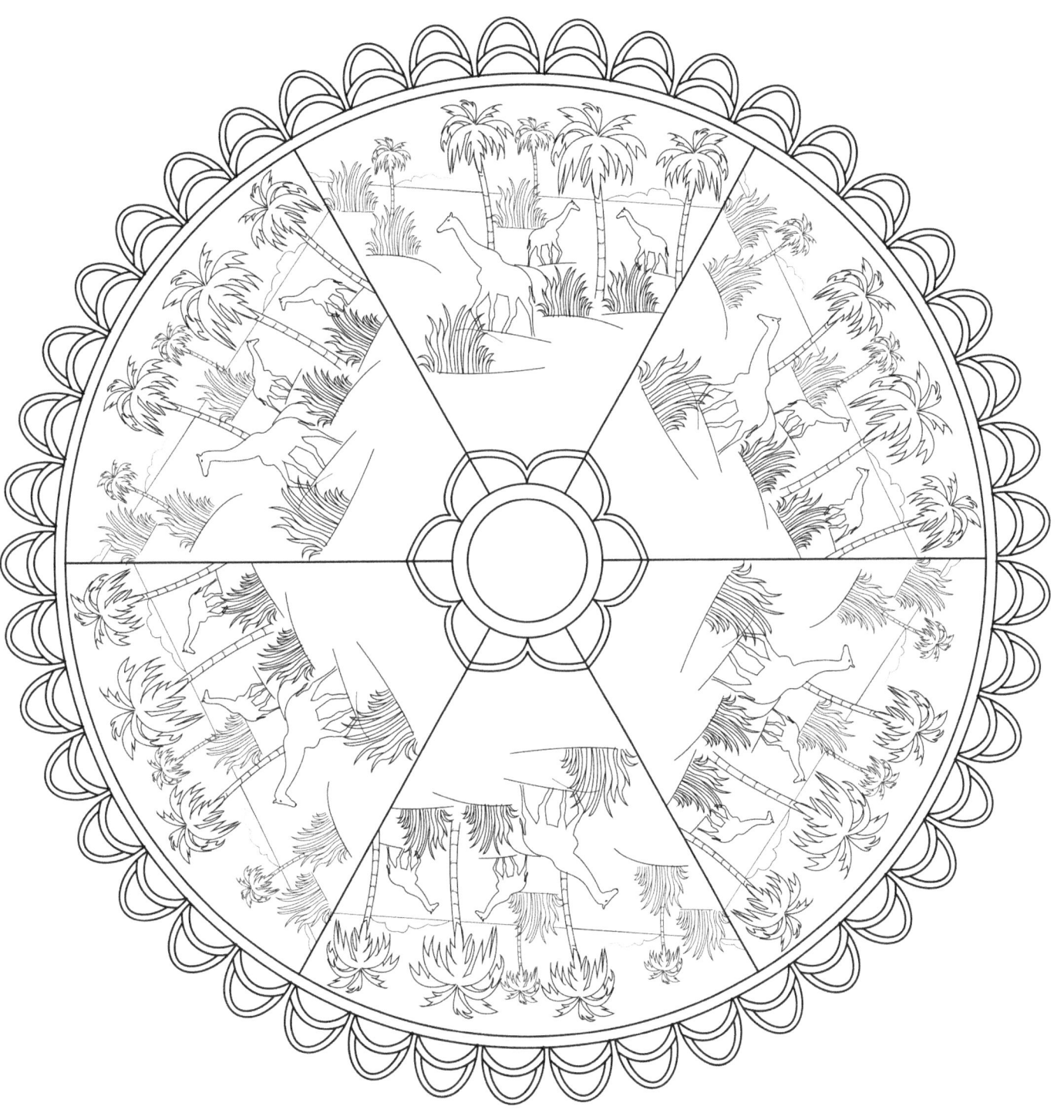

43

Make time
for the
quiet
moments,
as God
whispers
and the world
is loud.

(unknown)

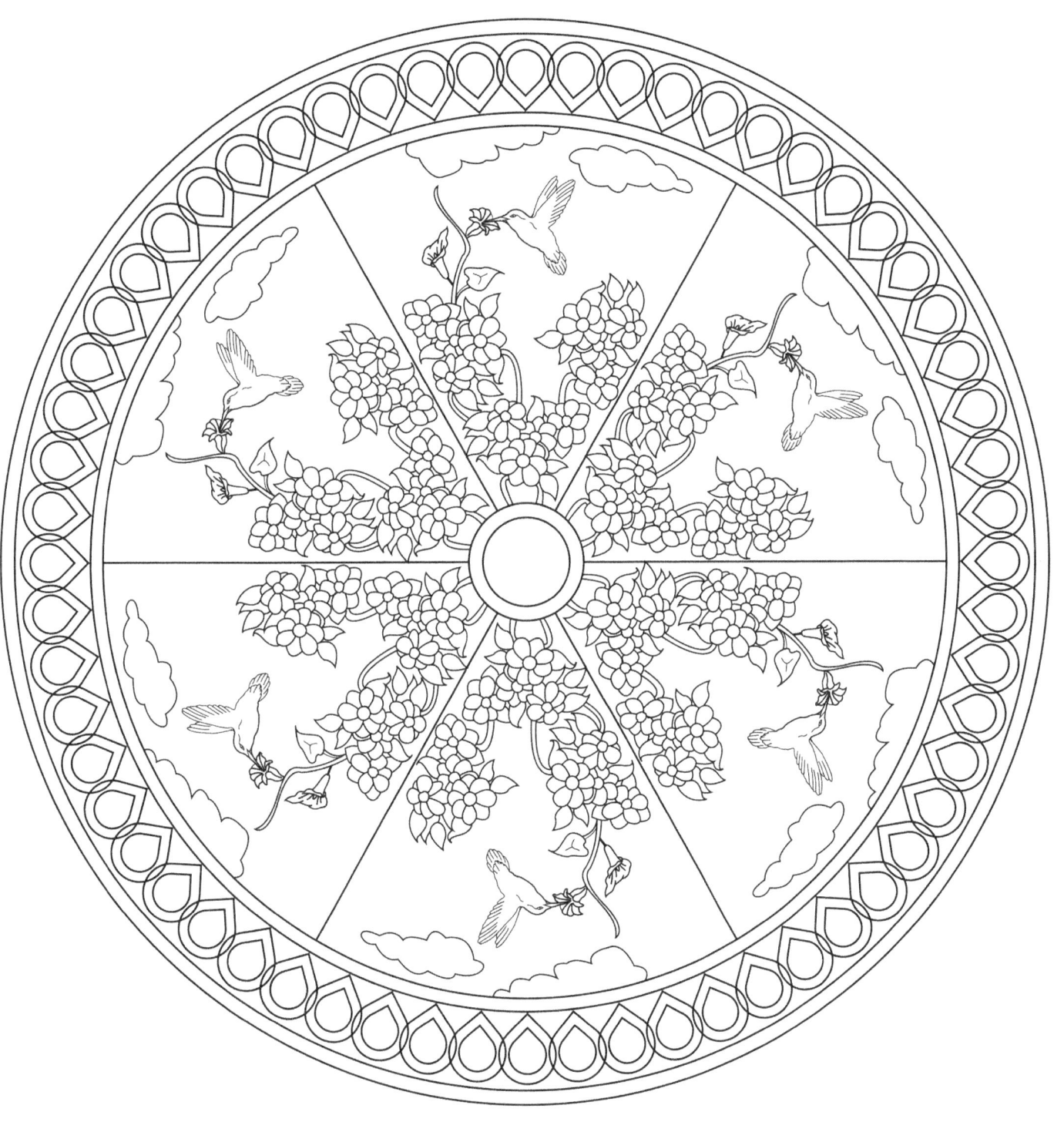

Every flower
is a soul
blossoming
in nature.

(Gerard De Nerval)

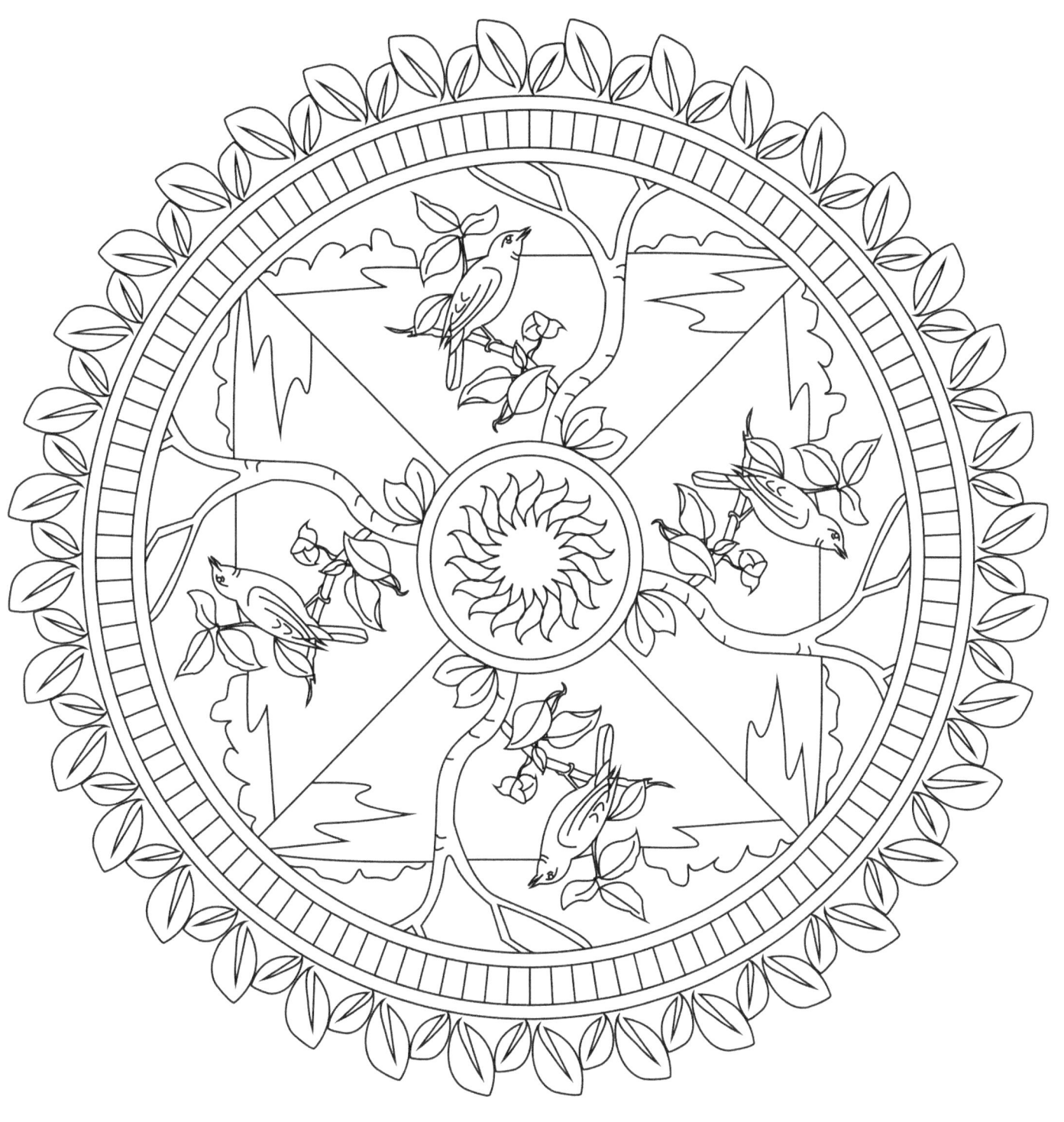

Meditation: Because some answers can only be found on the Inner net.

(Shira Tamir)

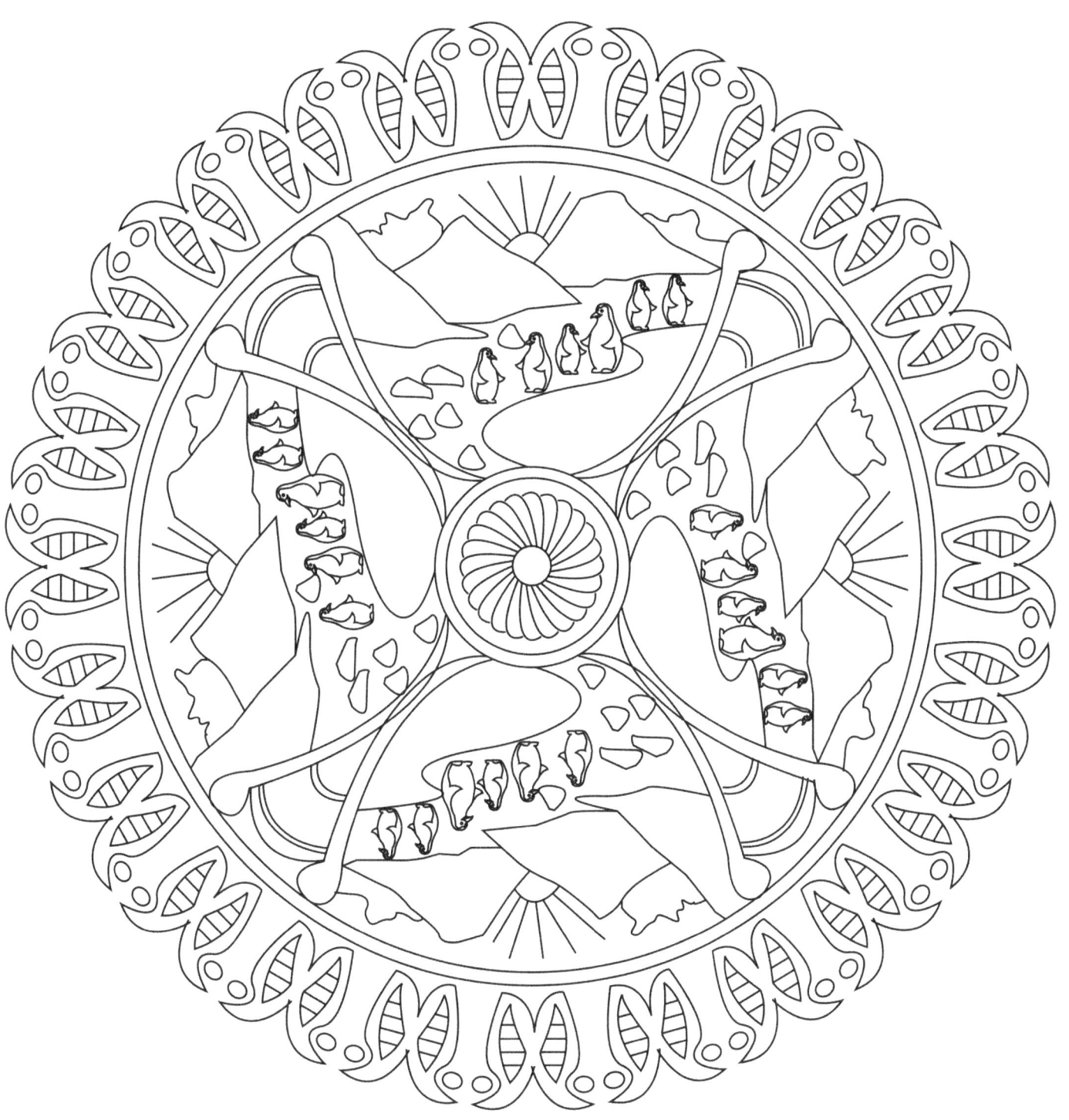

The journey
of a
thousand
miles
begins with
one step.

(Lao Tzu)

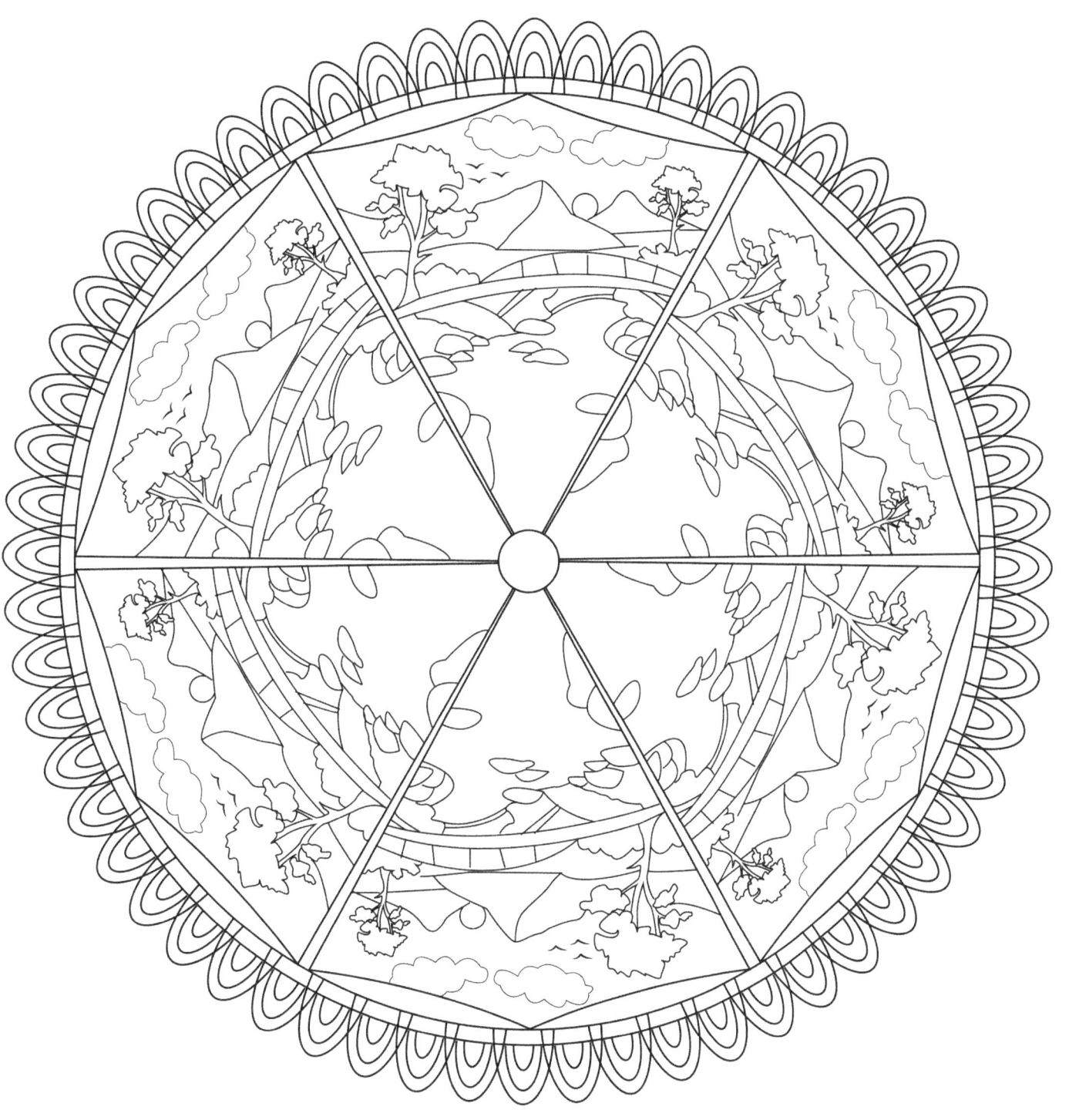

Happiness cannot be traveled to, owned, earned, or worn. It is the spiritual experience of living every minute with love, grace & gratitude.

(Denis Waitley)

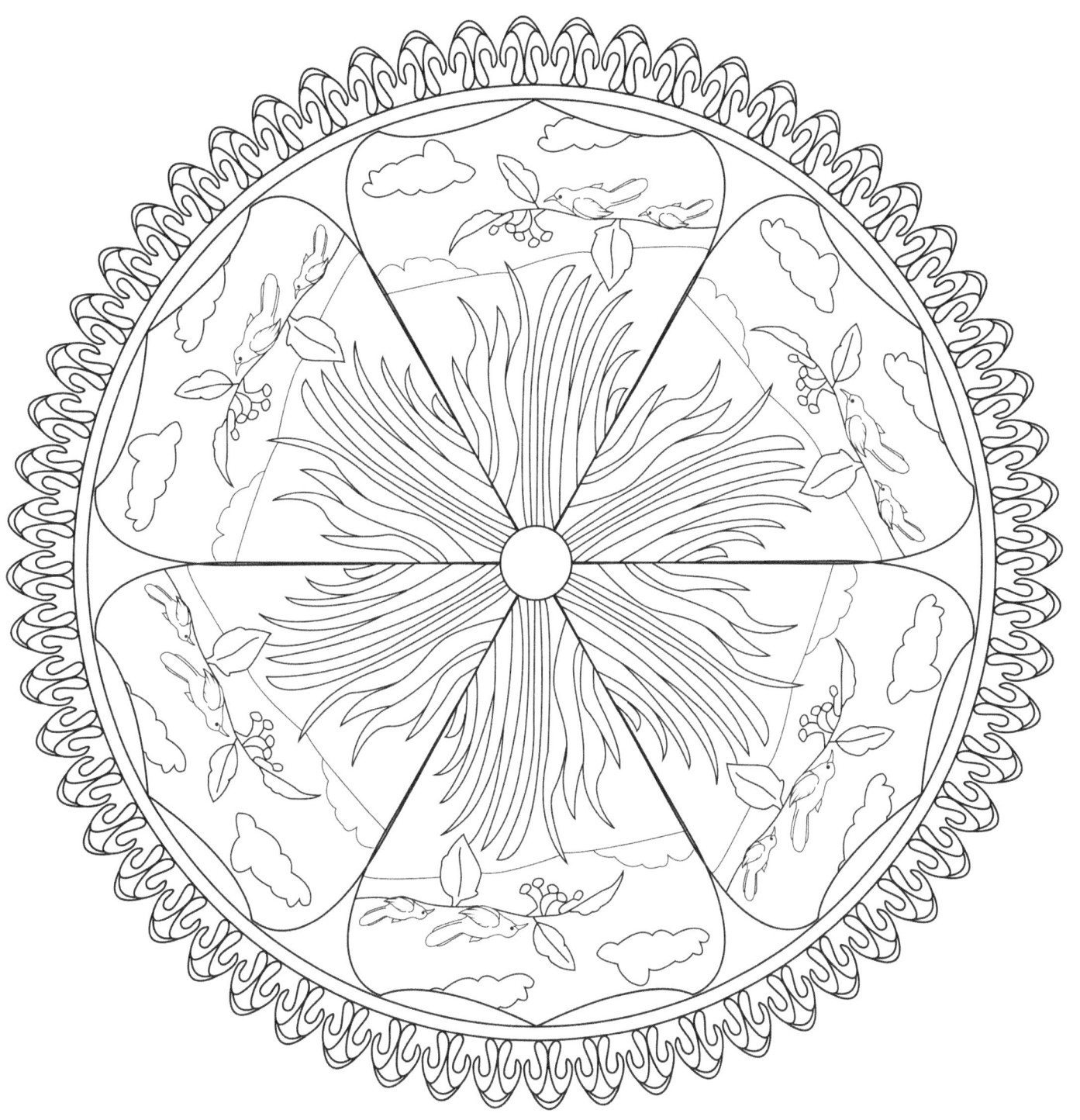

53

The best
dreams happen
when you're
awake.

(Cherie Gilderbloom)

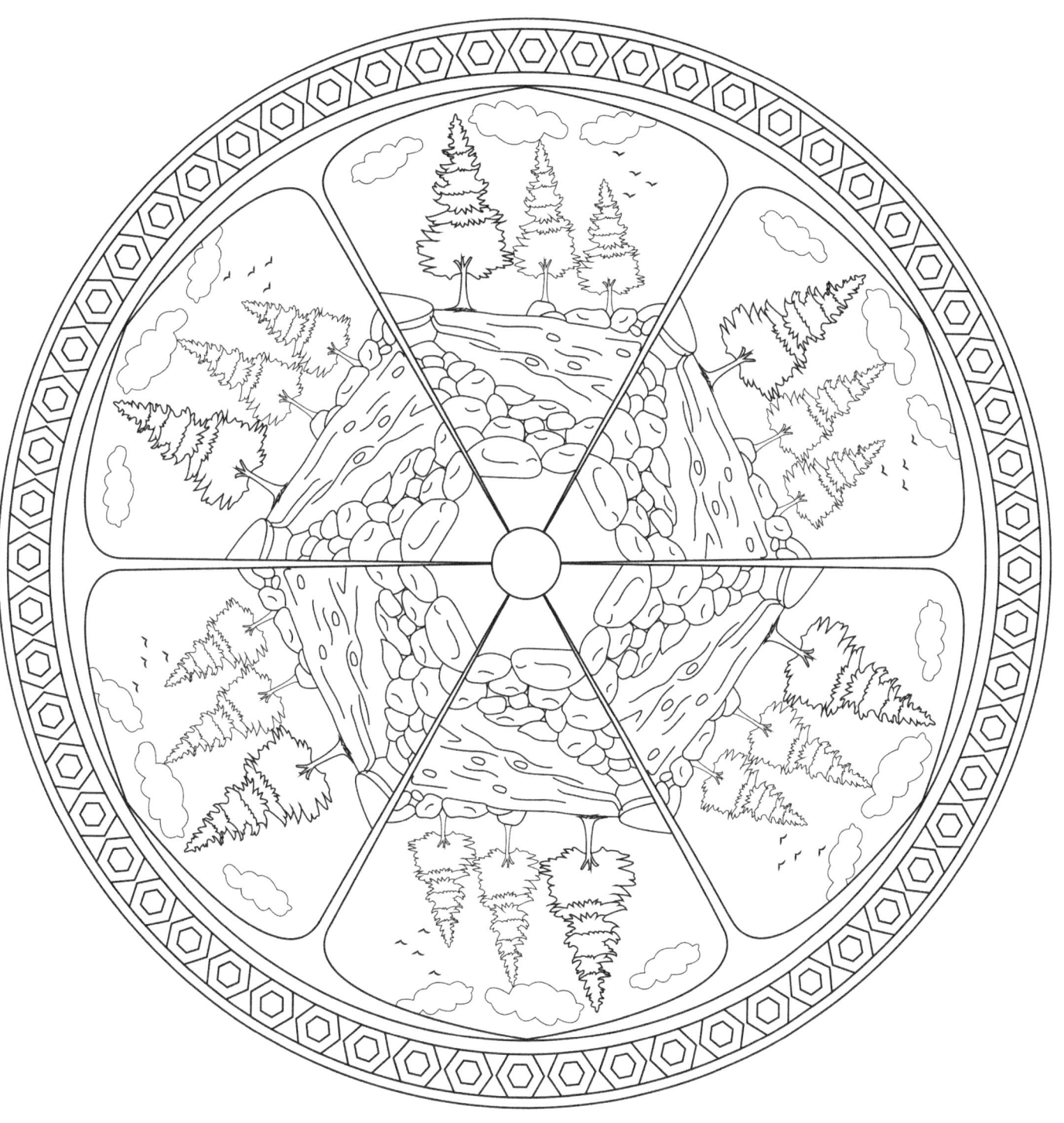

What art
offers
is space
- a certain
breathing
room for
the spirit.

(John Updike)

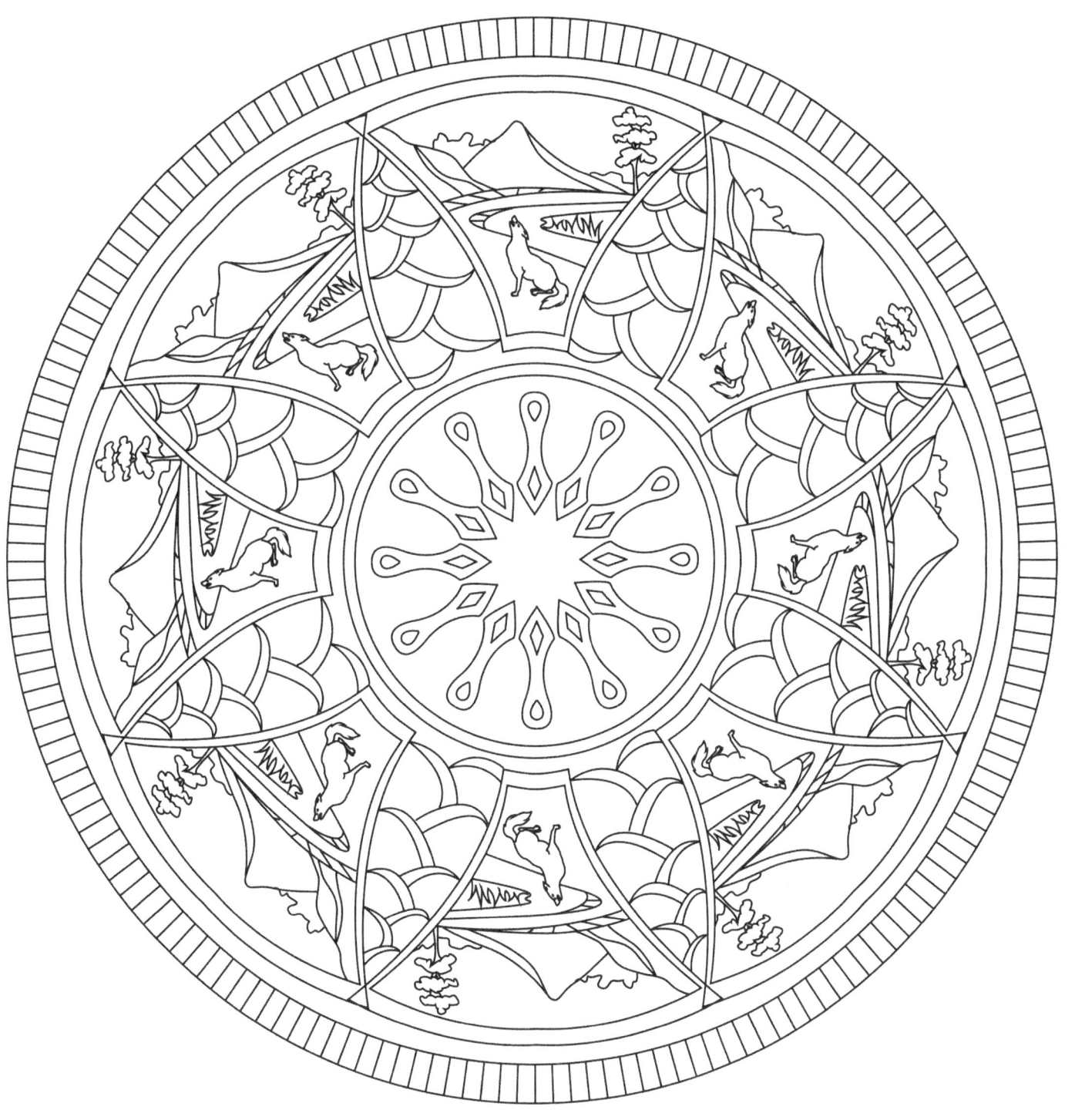

Whenever anyone has offended me, I try to raise my soul so high that the offense cannot reach it.

(Rene Descartes)

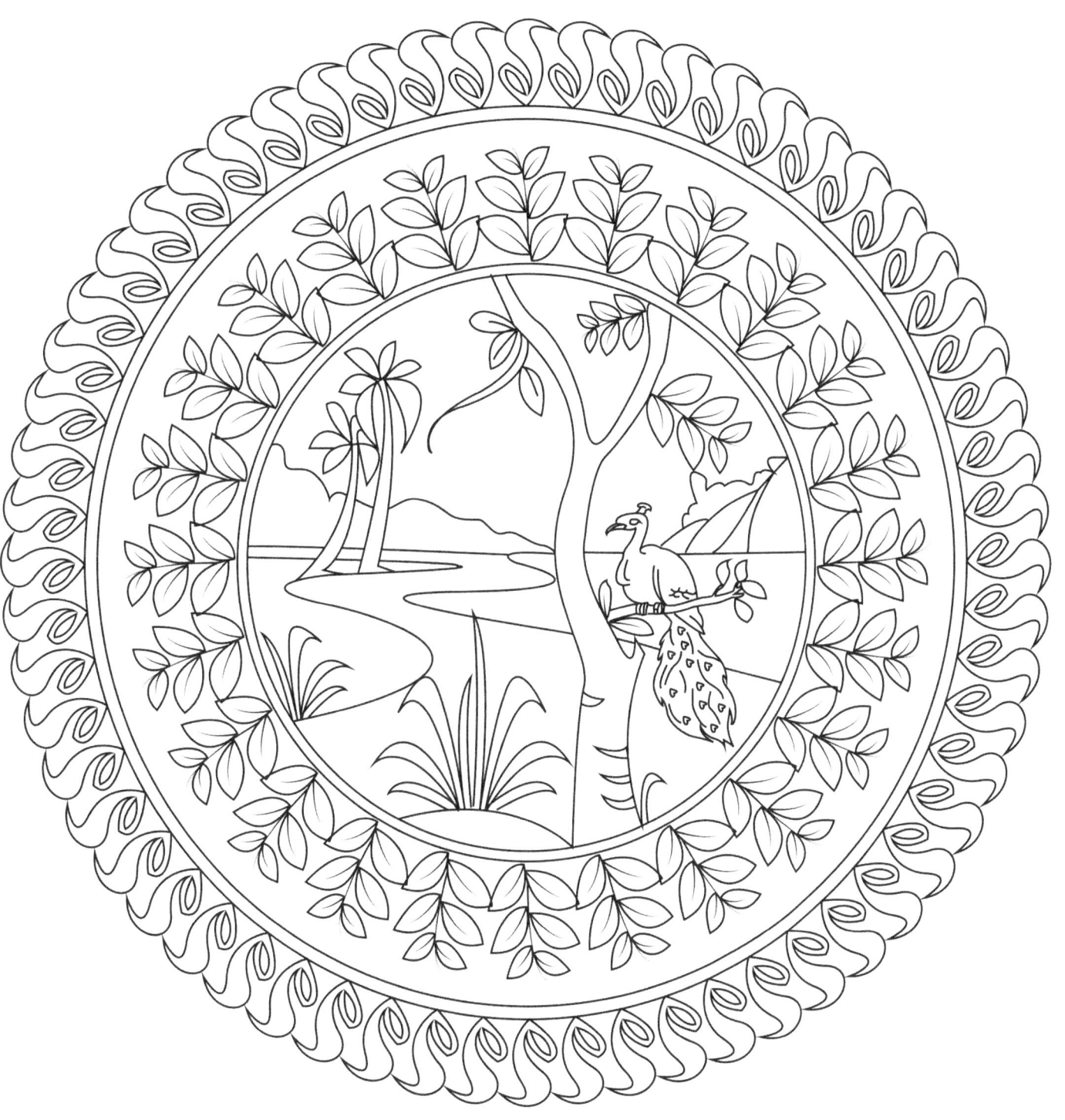

A work of art
is above all
an adventure
of the mind.

(Eugene Ionesco)

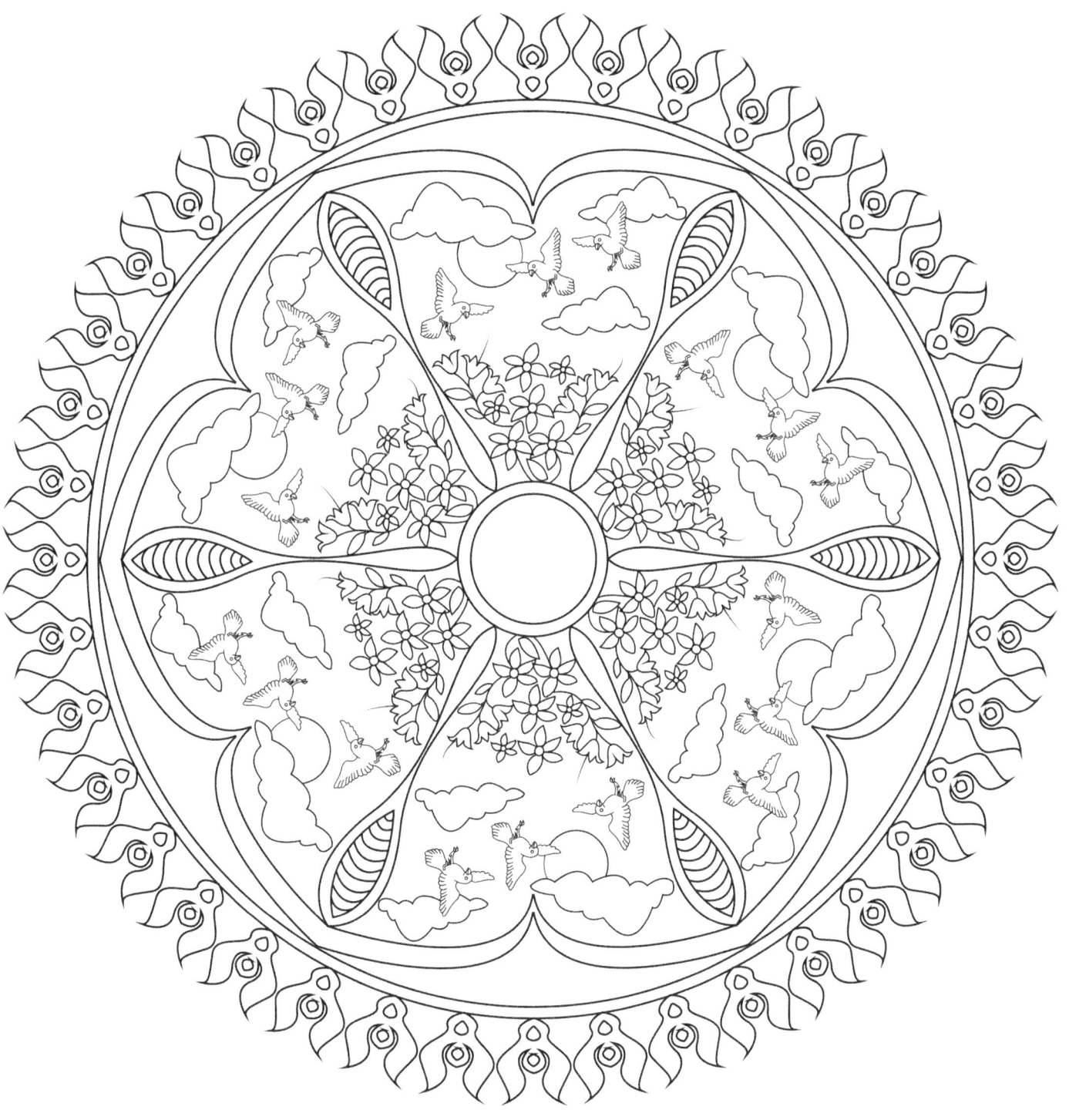

If you hear a voice within you say 'you cannot paint,' then by all means paint, and that voice will be silenced.

(Vincent Van Gogh)

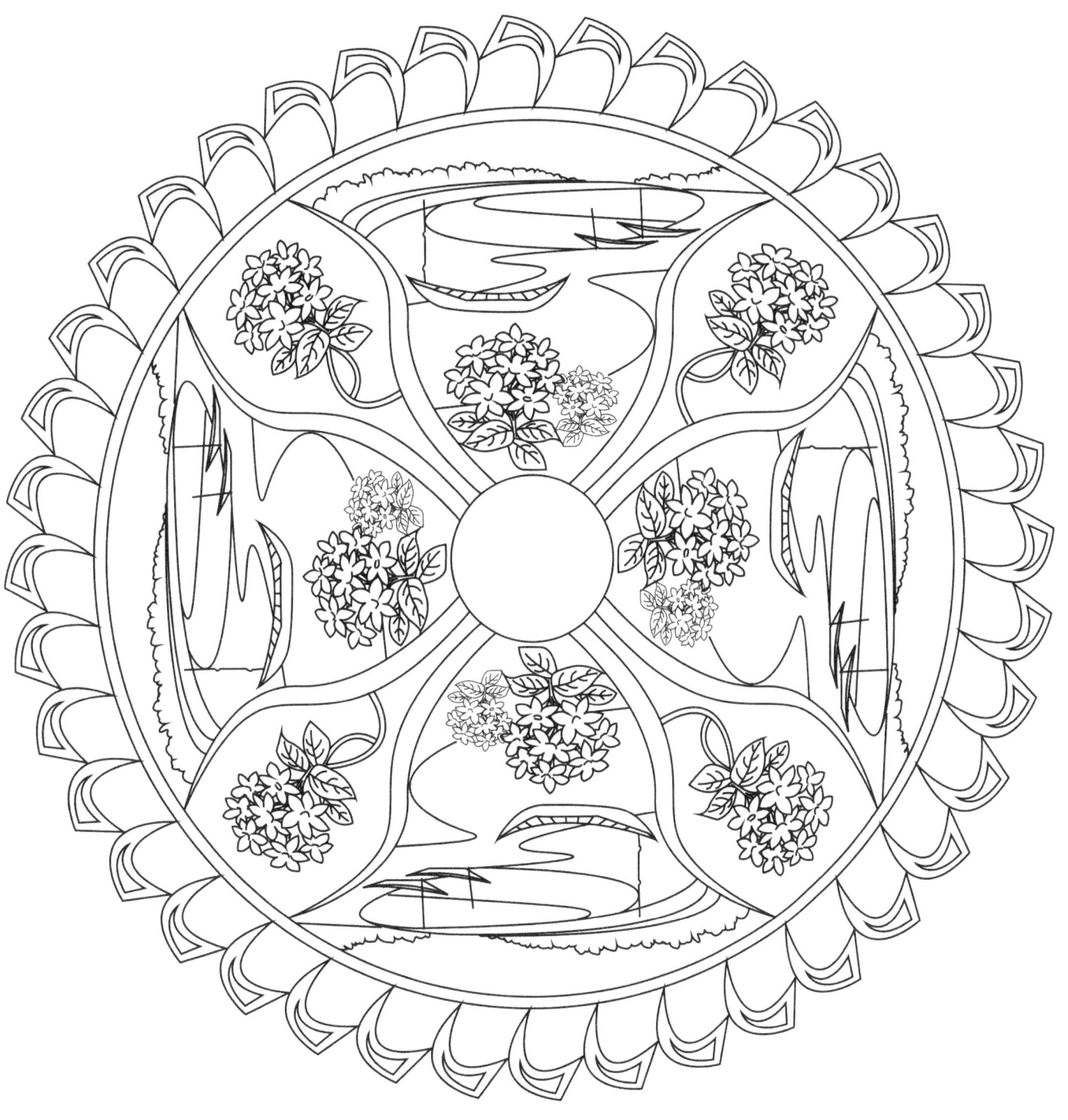

Knowing yourself is the beginning of all wisdom.

(Aristotle)

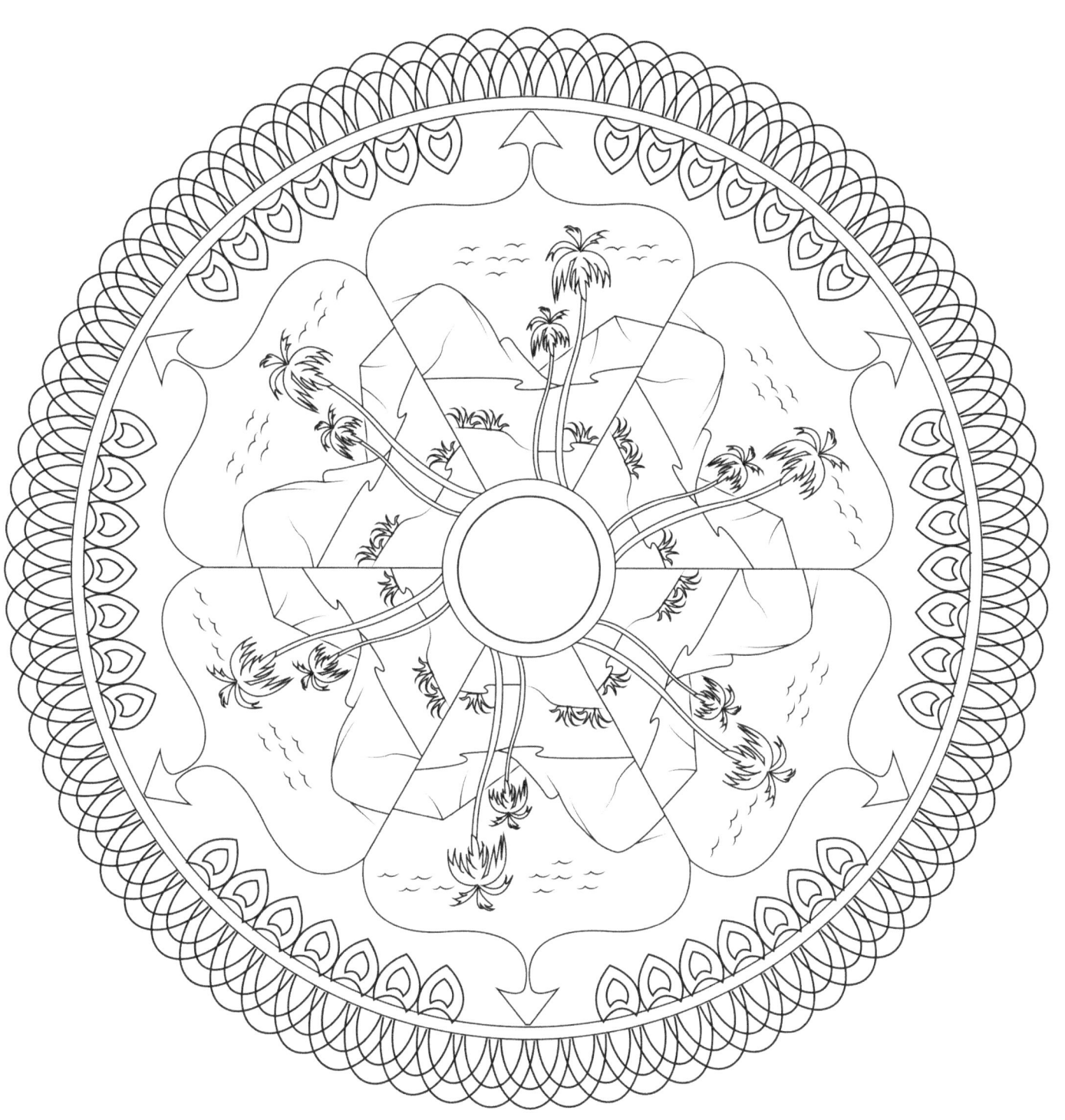

Man is free
at the
moment
he wishes
to be.

(Voltaire)

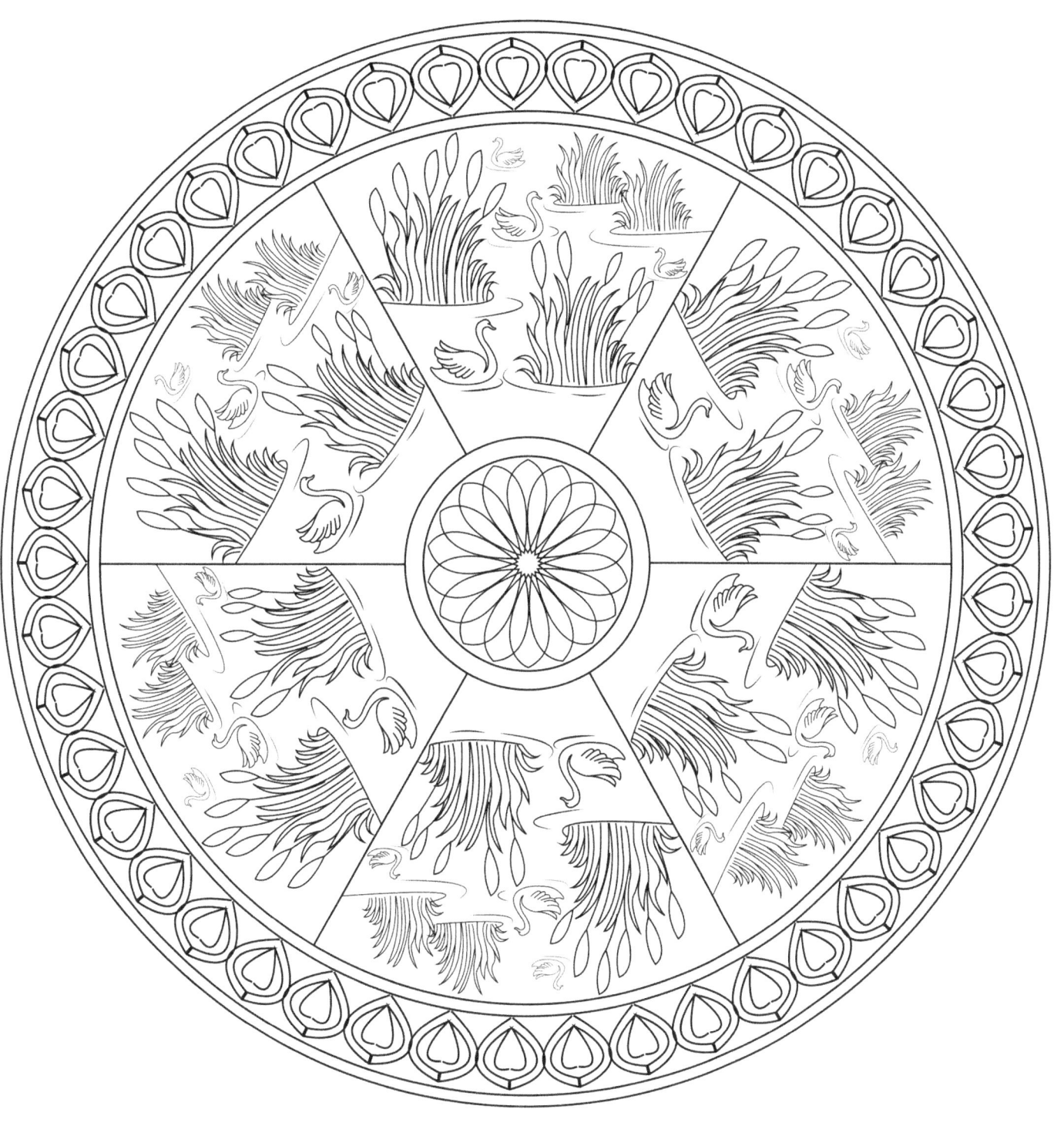

67

Vision
is the art
of seeing
what is
invisible
to others.

(Jonathan Swift)

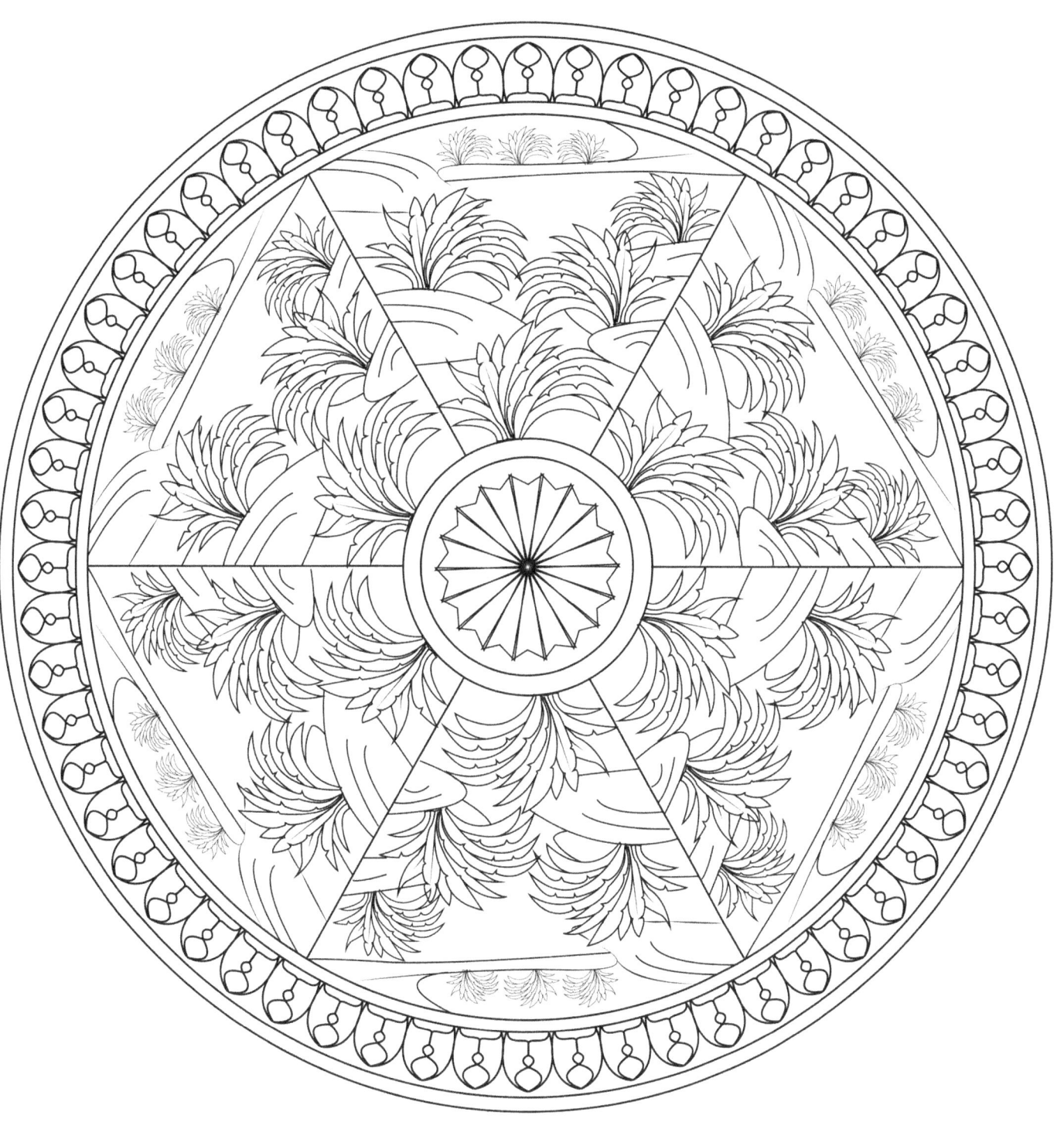

69

Art
is a
harmony
parallel
with
nature.

(Paul Cezanne)

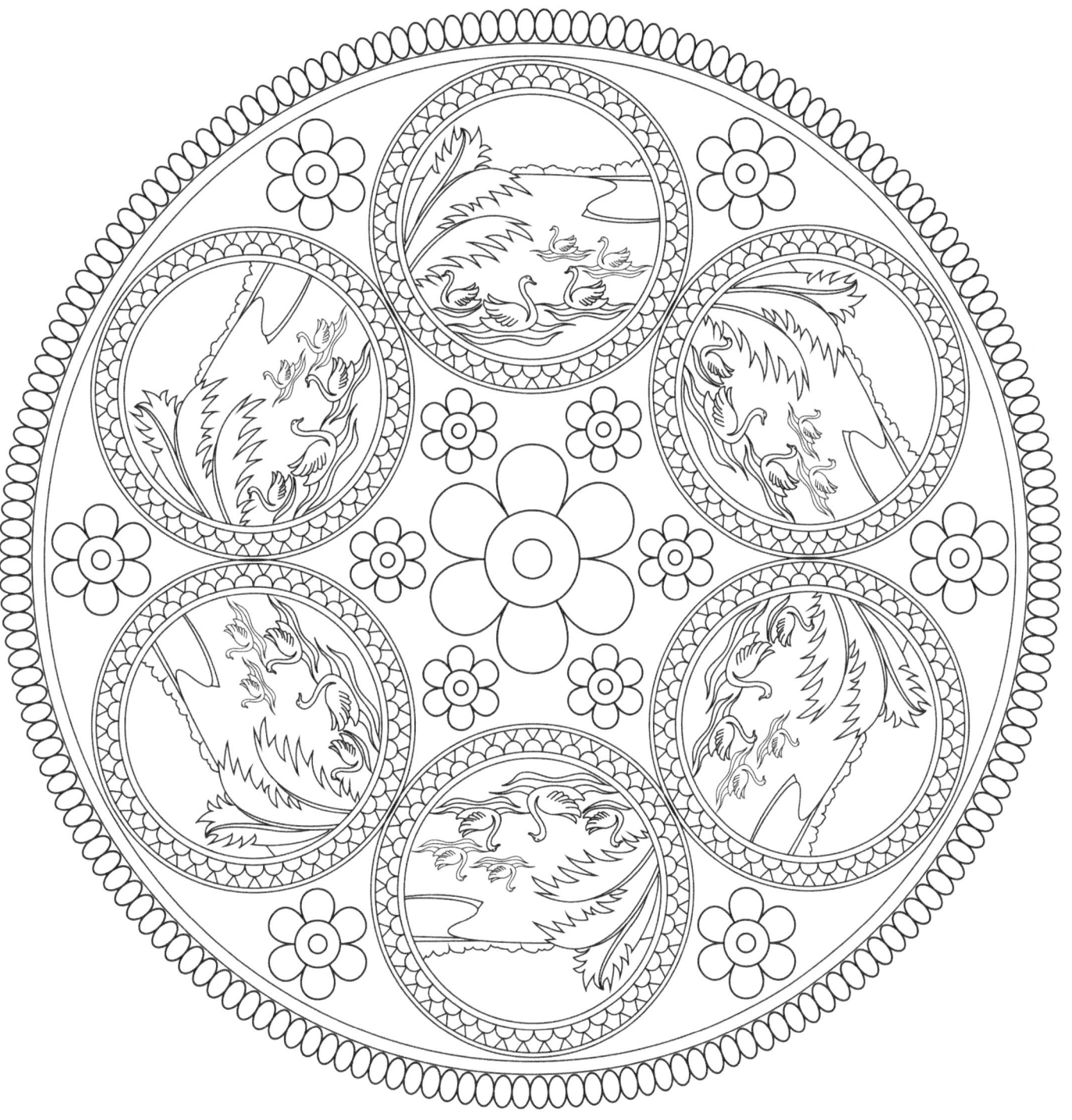

71

Change
your thoughts
and you
change your
world.

(Norman Vincent Peale)

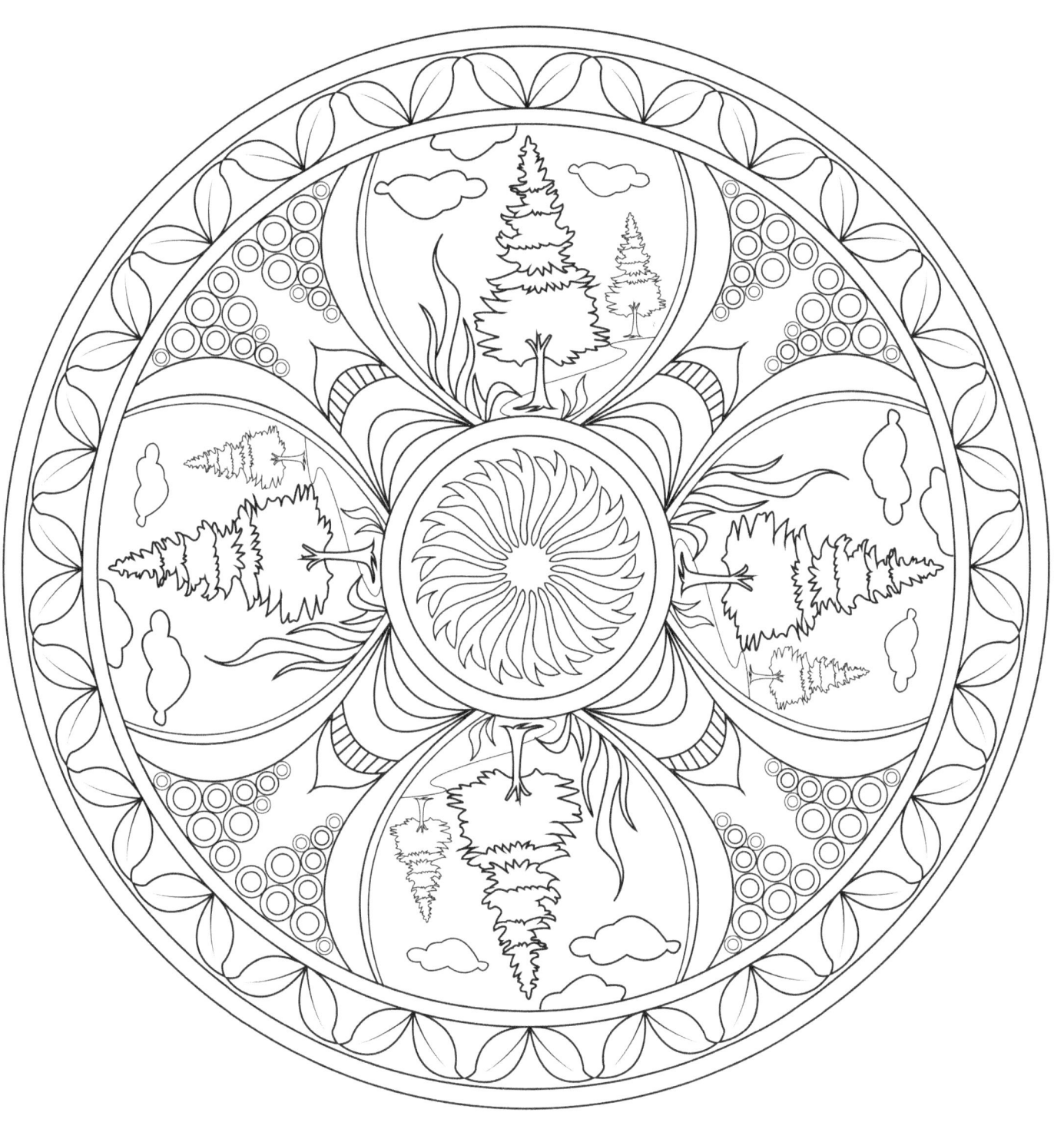

73

The best way
to predict
the future
is to
invent it.

(Alan Kay)

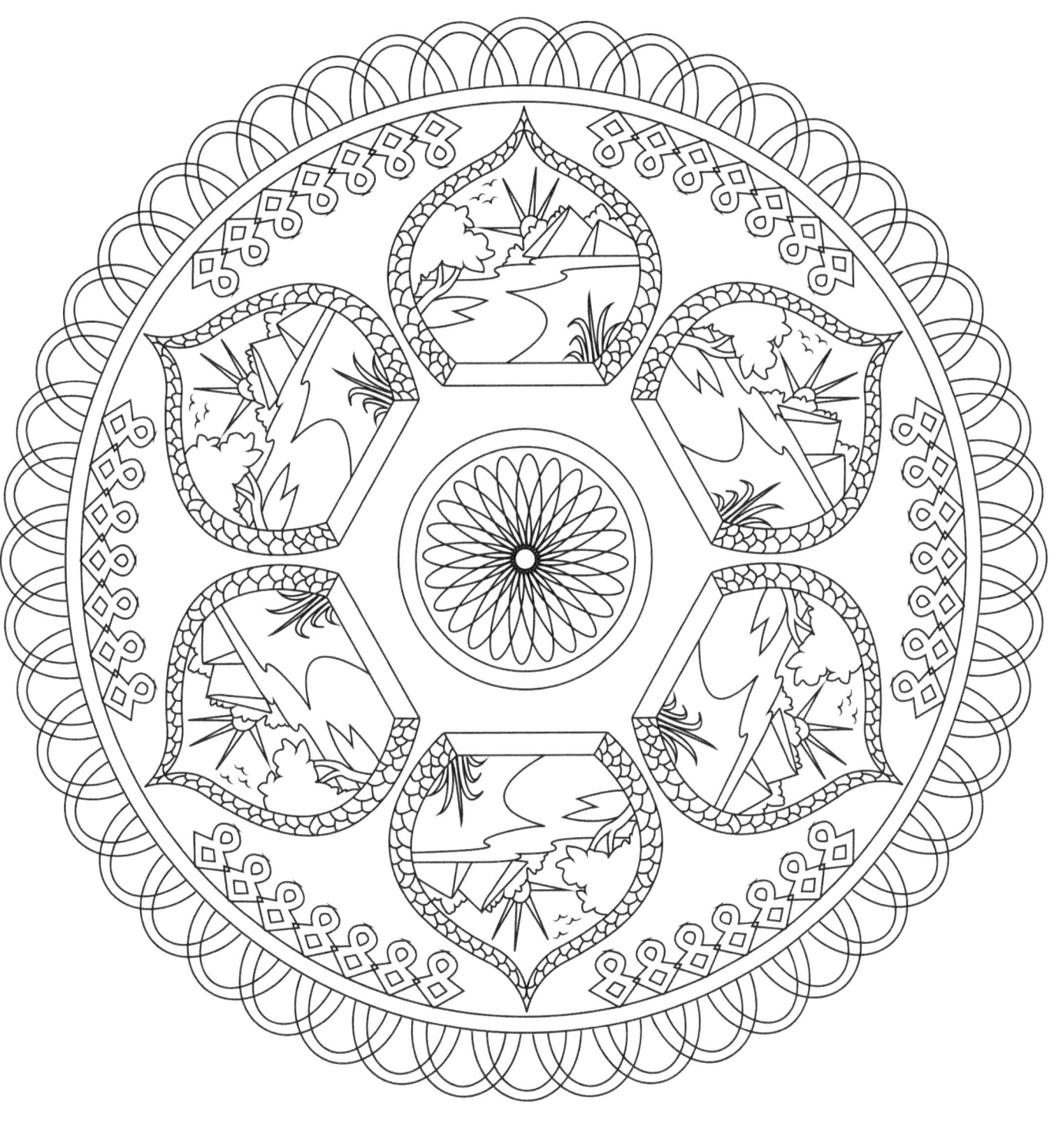

I have been
a seeker and
I still am,
but I stopped
asking
the books
and the
stars.
I started
listening
to the
teaching of
my Soul.

(Rumi)

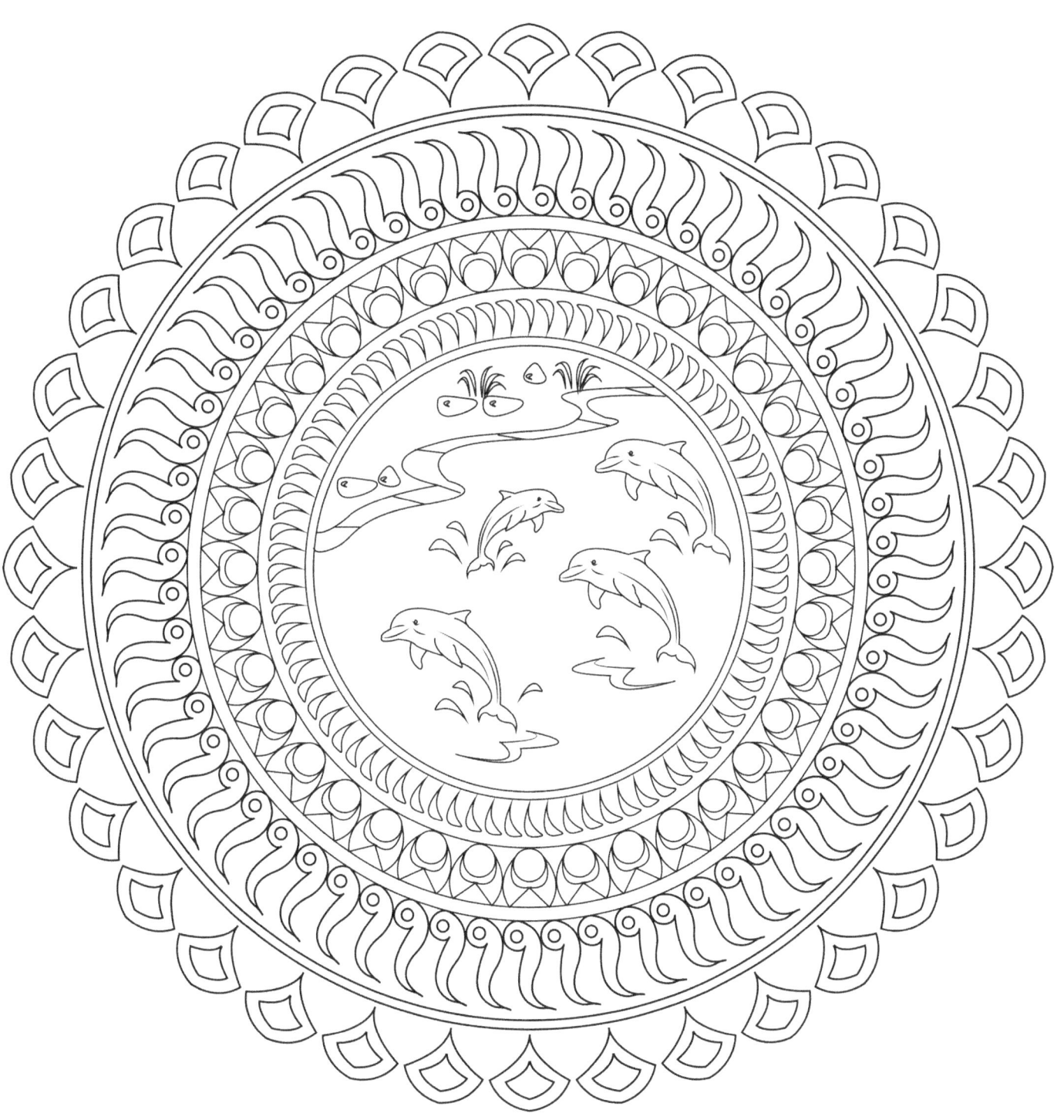

Looking
at beauty in
the world,
is the first
step of
purifying
the mind.

(Amit Ray)

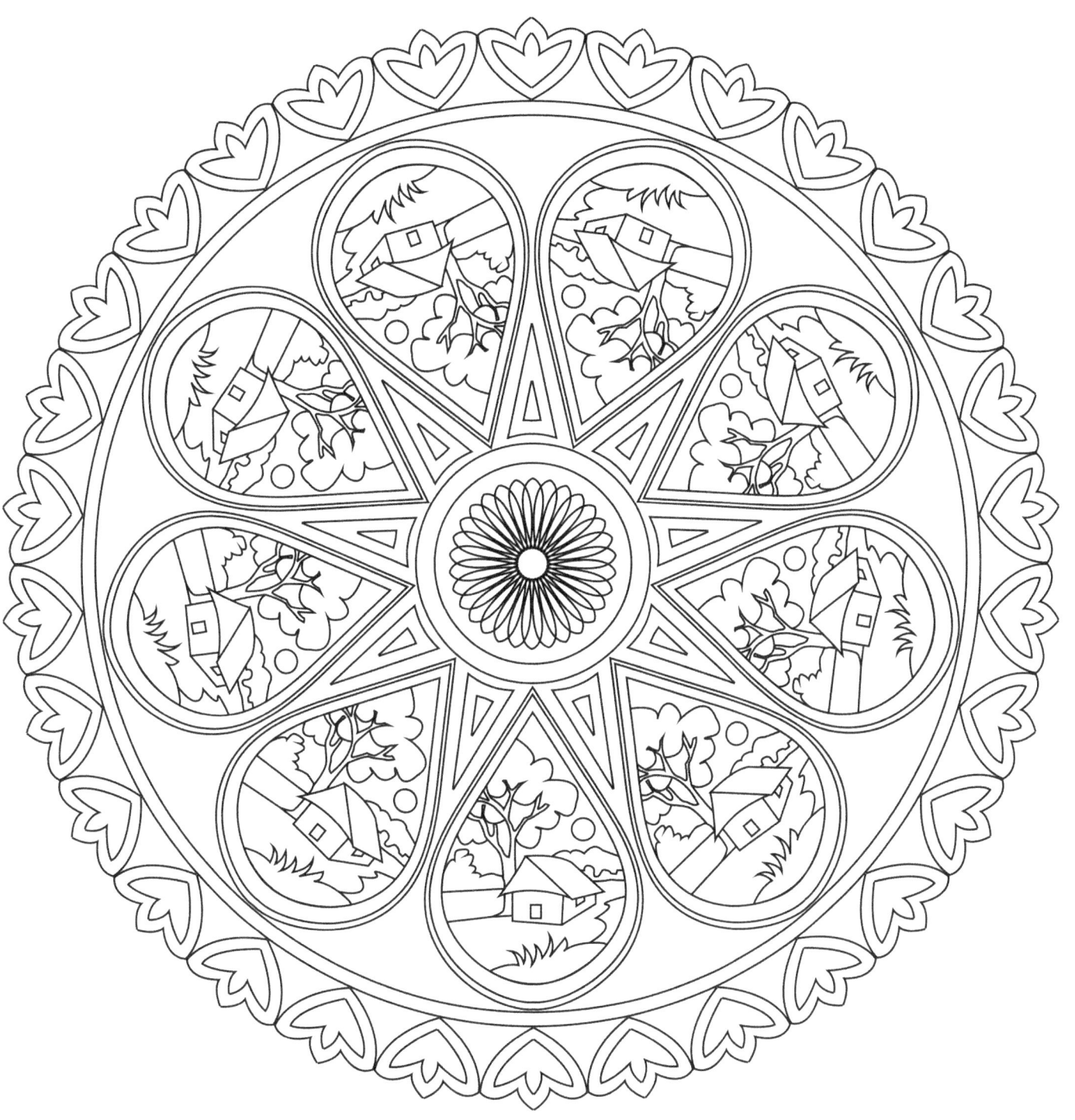

May you live
all the days
of your life.

(Jonathan Swift)

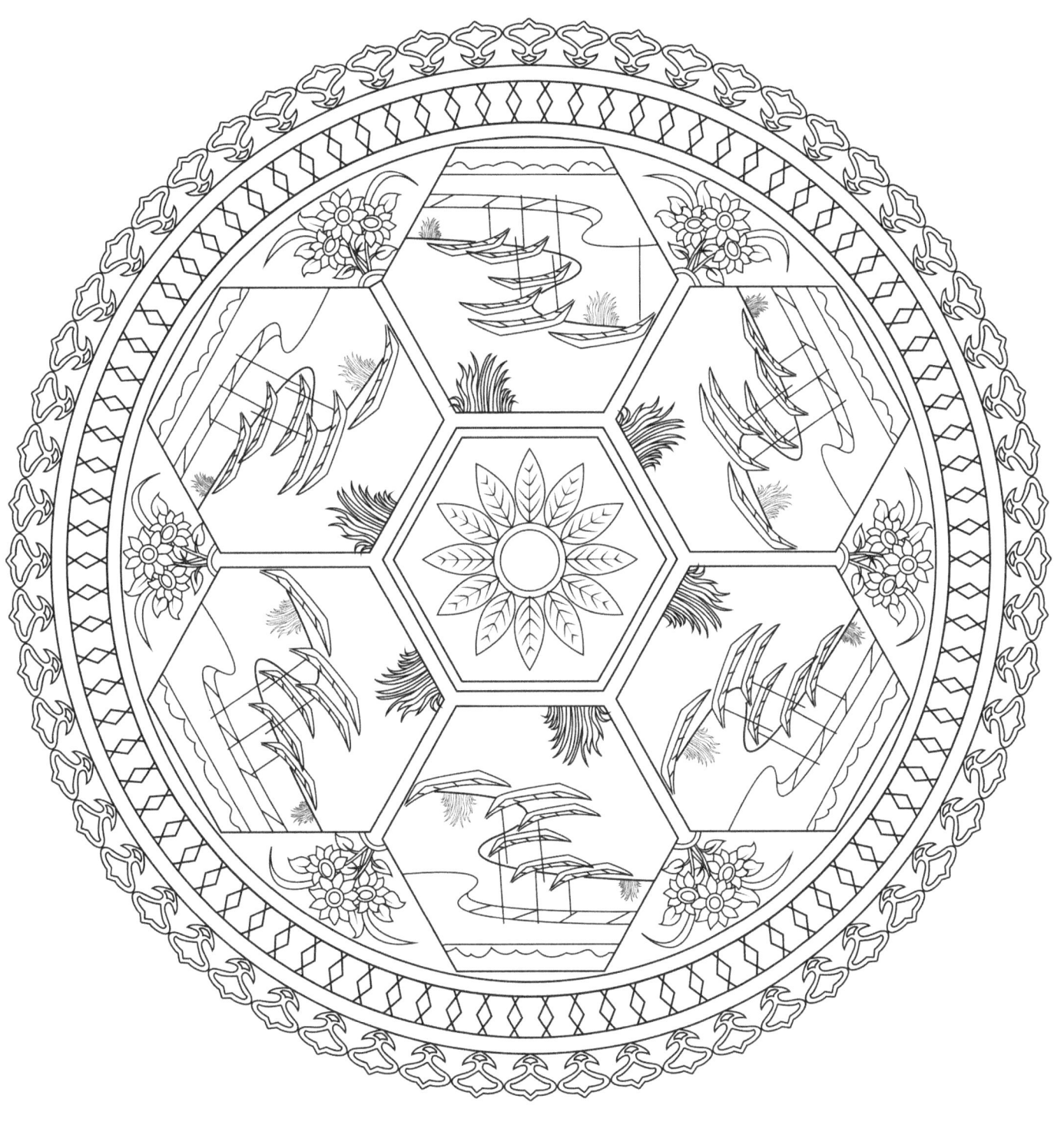

81

It's a
good idea
always to do
something
relaxing
prior to
making an
important
decision in
your life.

(Paulo Coelho)

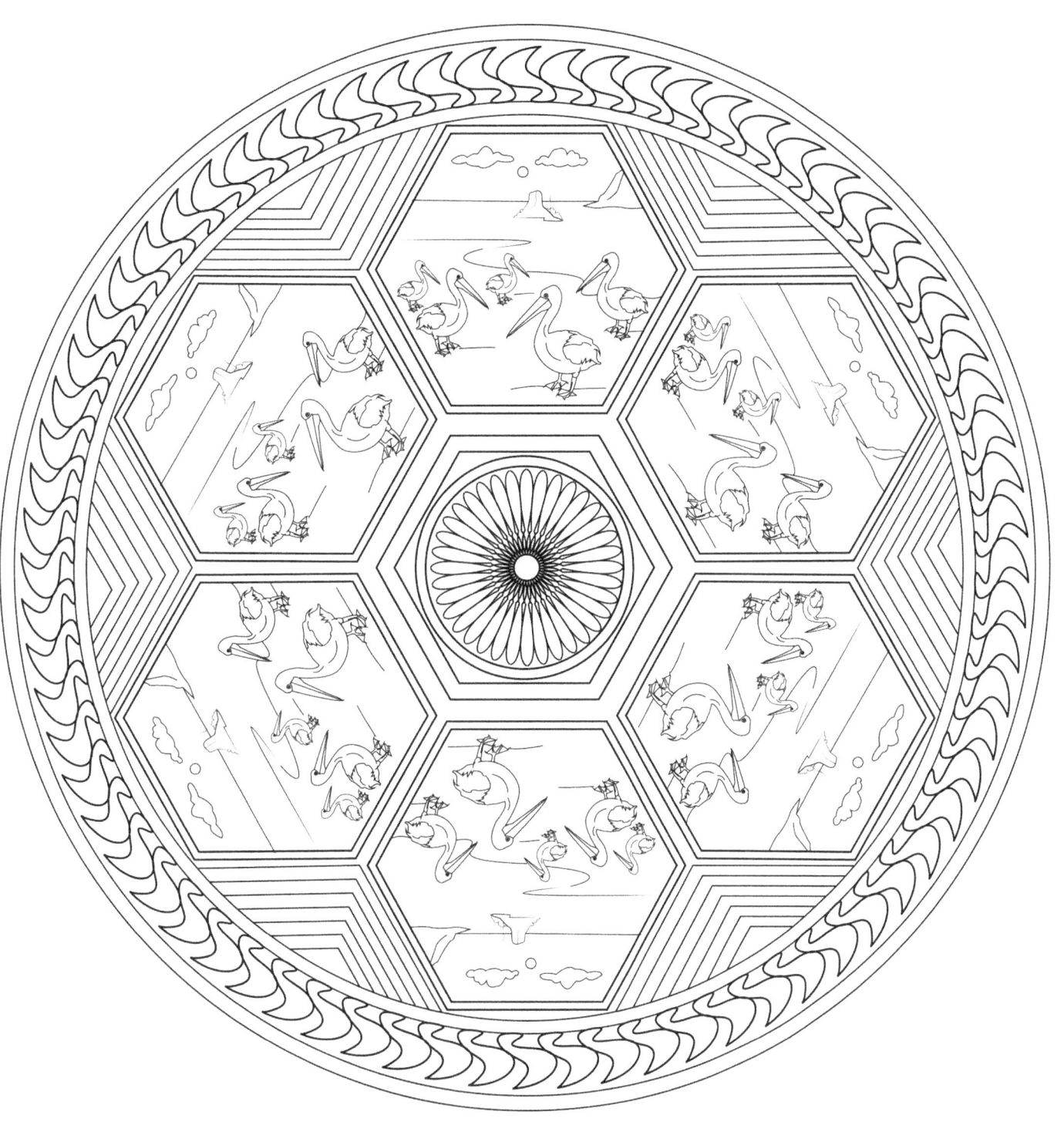

Imagination is more important than knowledge.

(Albert Einstein)

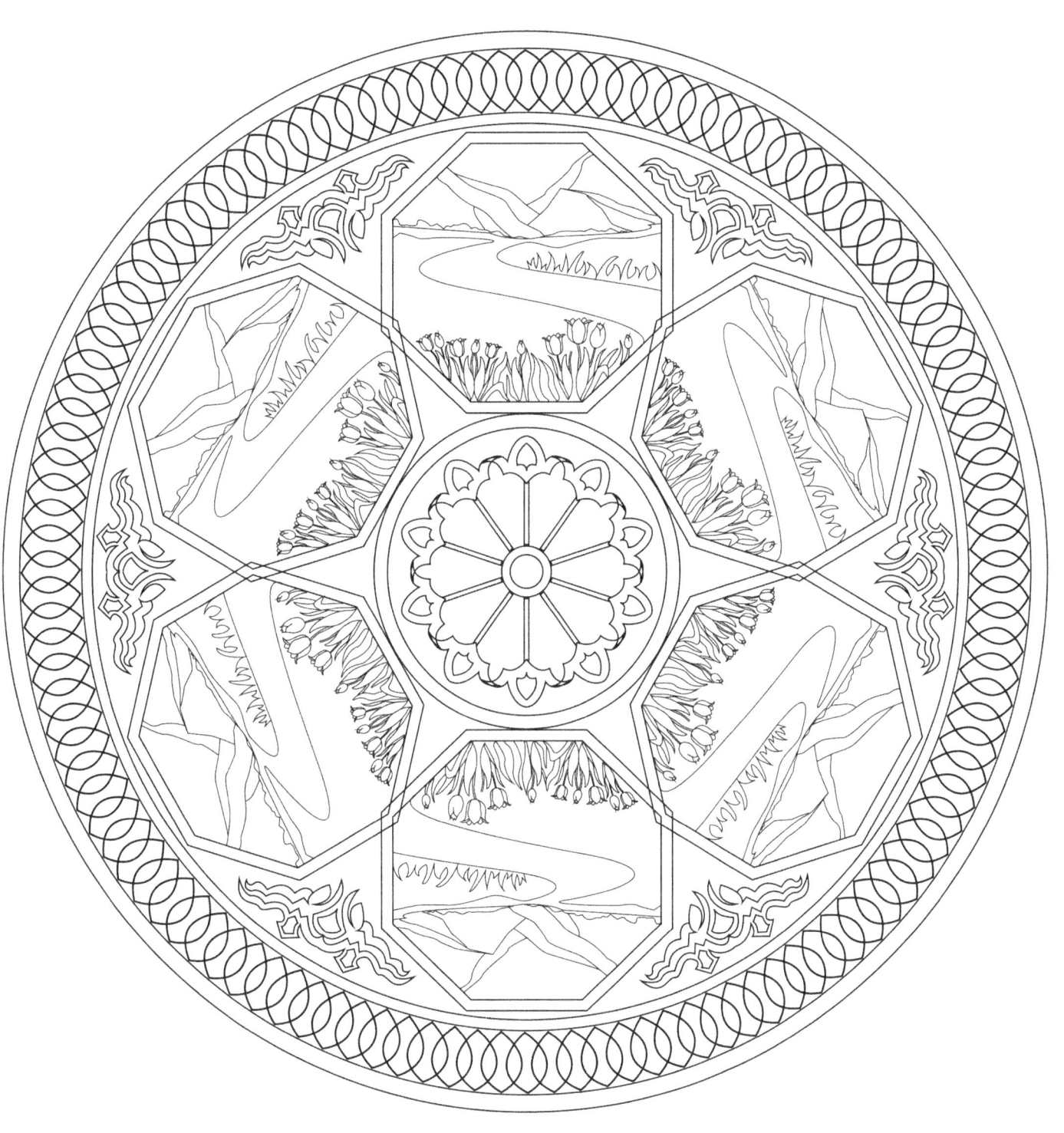

Meditation is listening to the Divine within.

(Edgar Cayce)

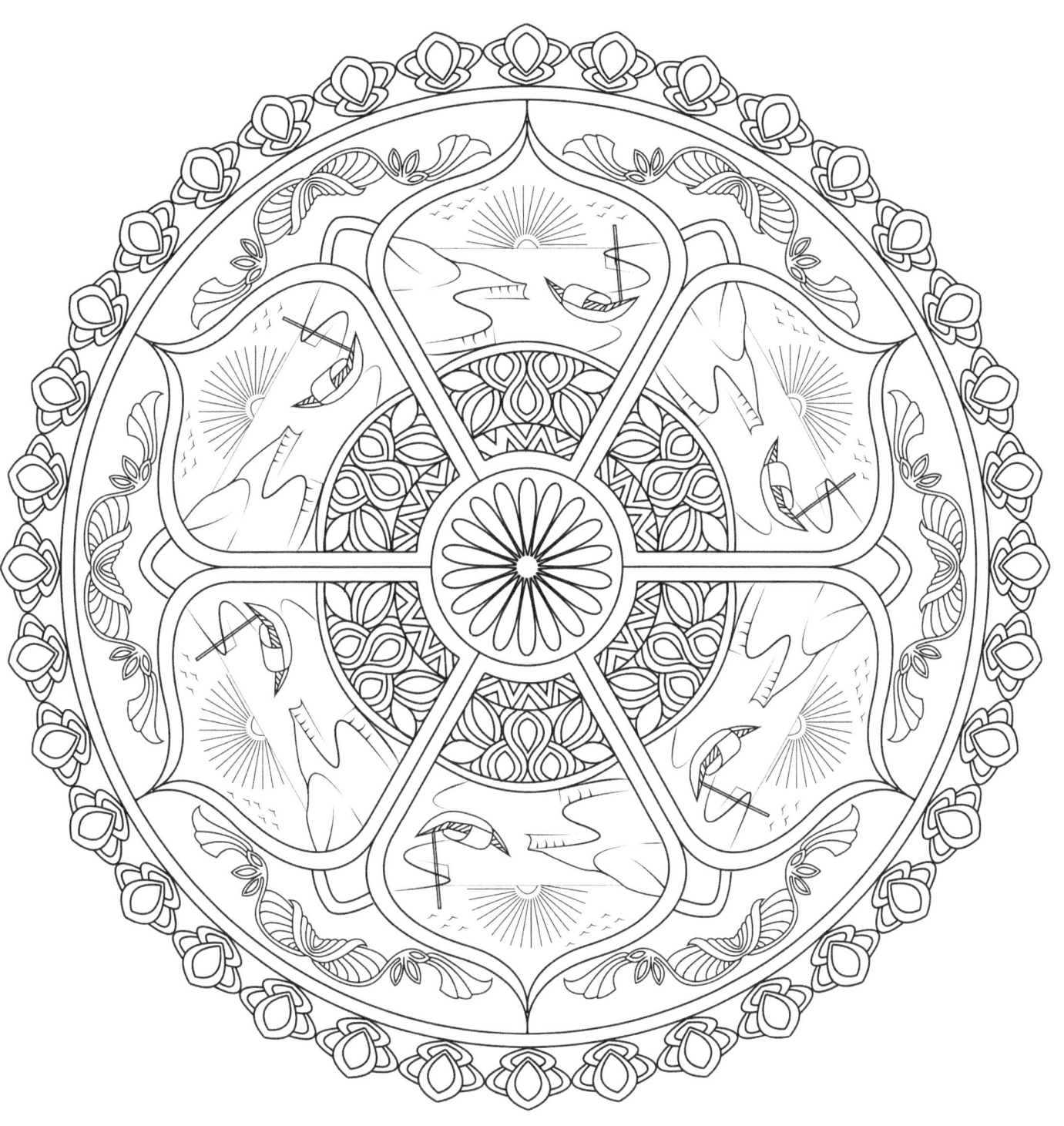

Life is not
a problem
to be solved,
but a reality
to be
experienced .

(Soren Kierkegaard)

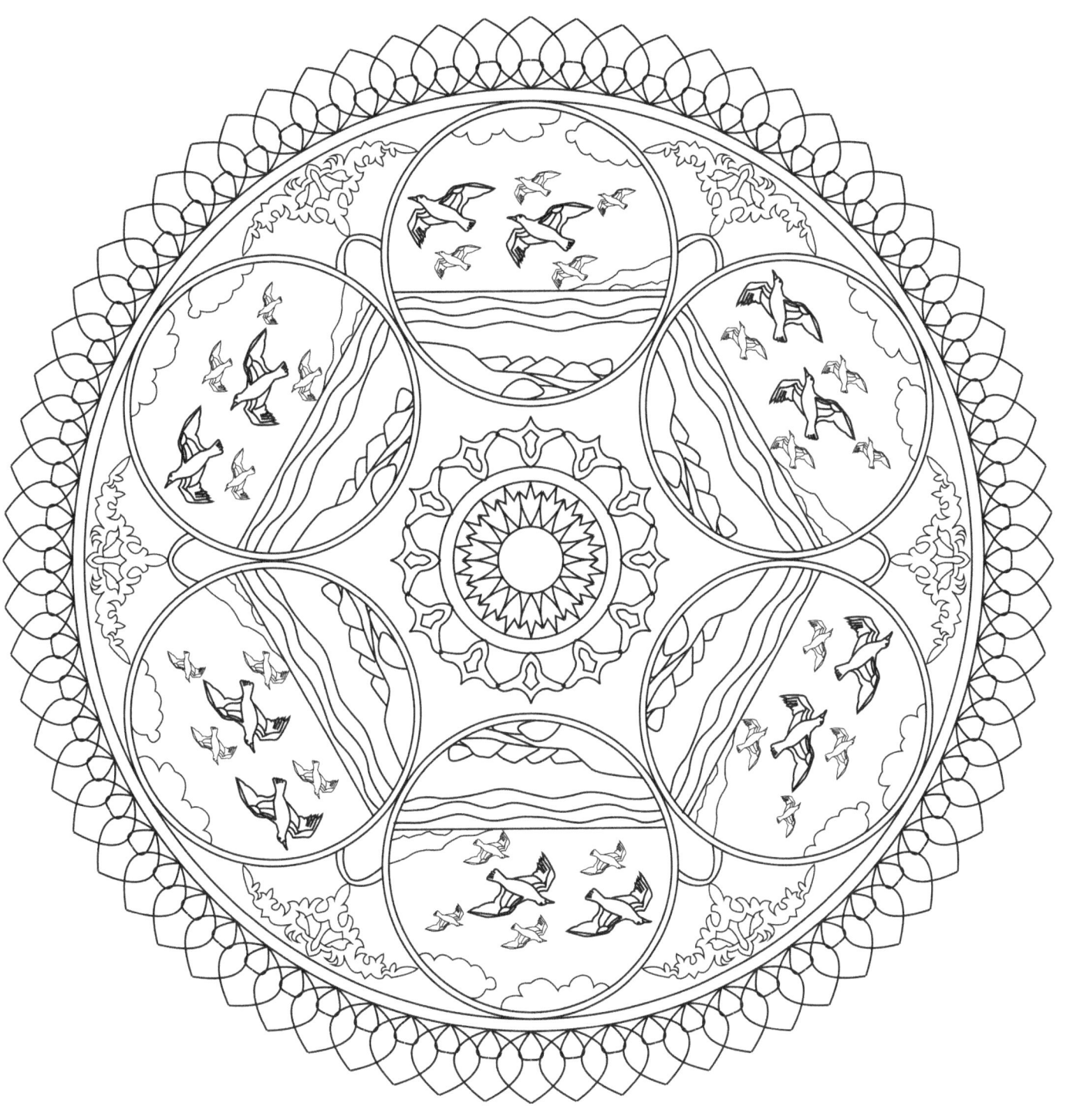

Limitations live only in our minds. But if we use our imaginations, our possibilities become limitless.

(Jamie Paolinetti)

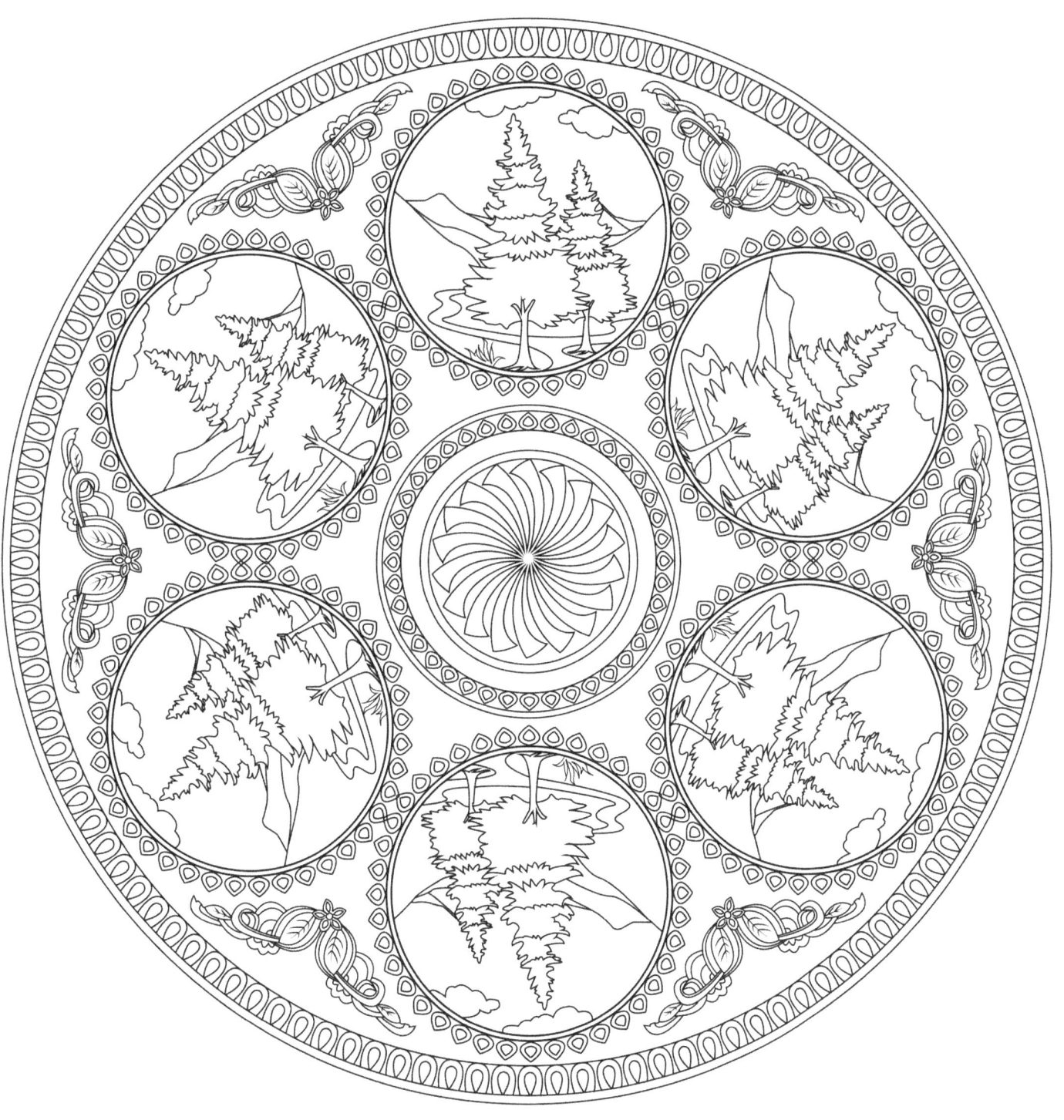

The creation
of a thousand
forests is in
one acorn.

(Ralph Waldo Emerson)

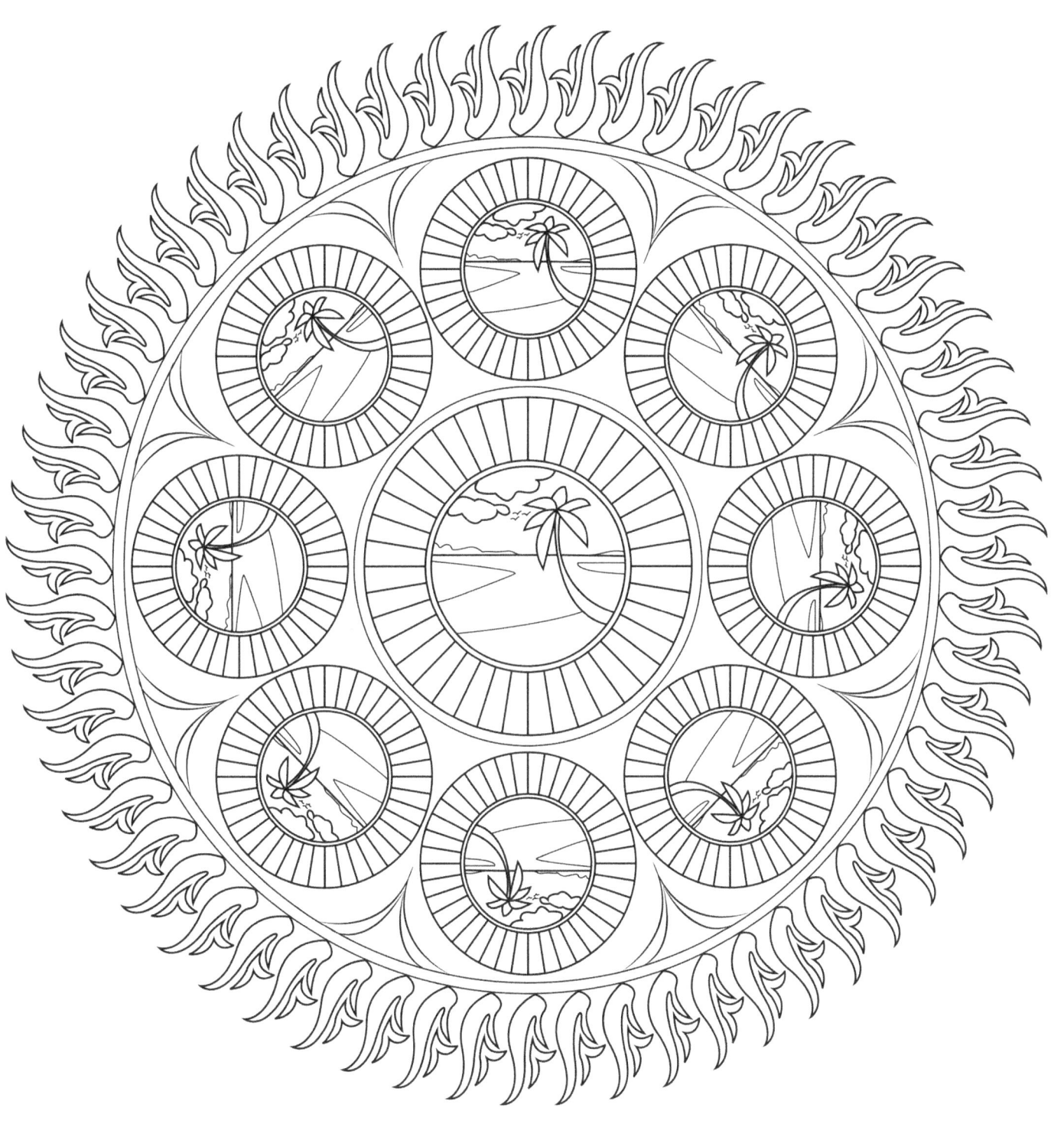

Art is
the daughter
of freedom.

(Friedrich Schiller)

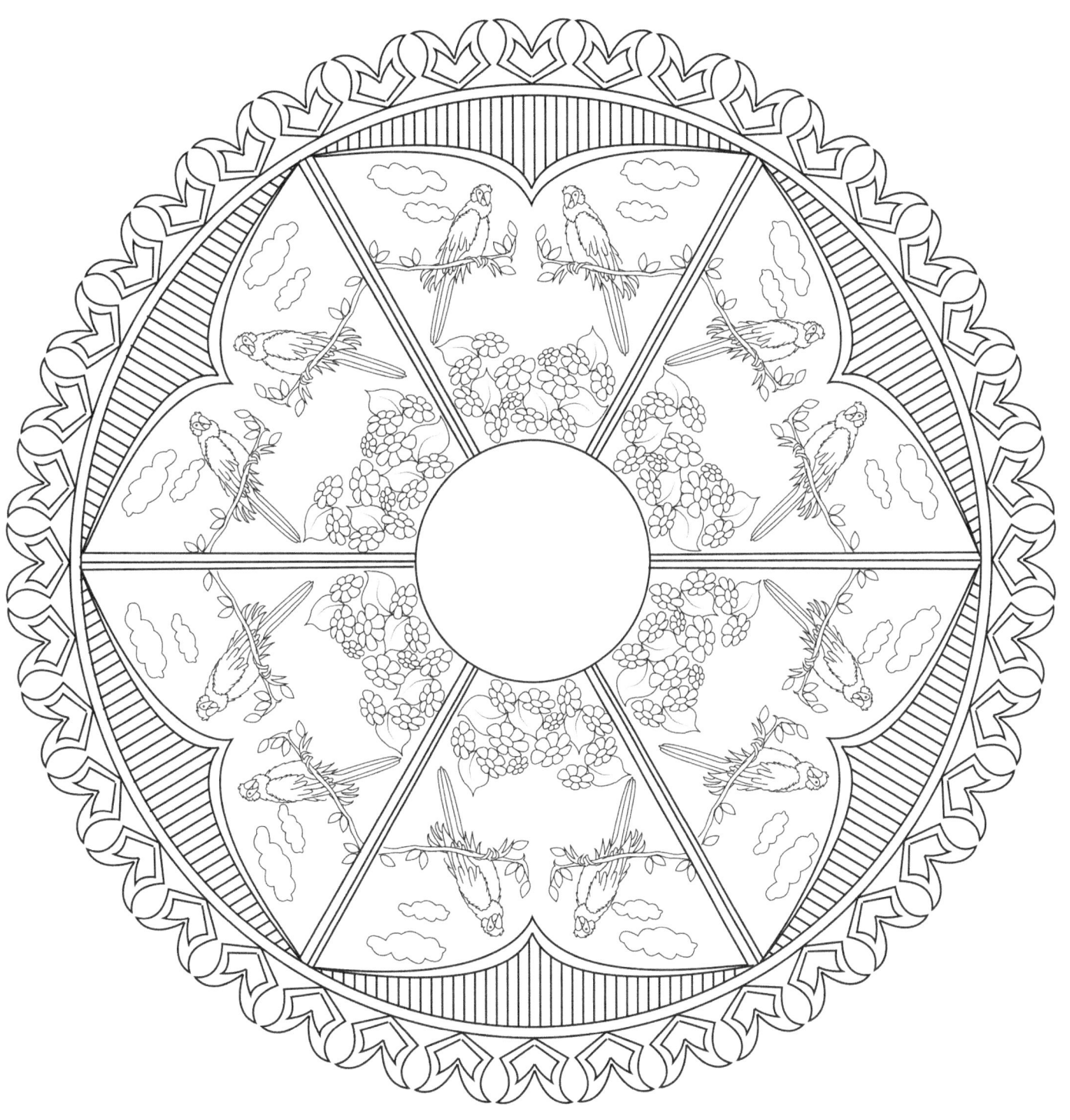

The more
man
meditates
upon good
thoughts,
the better
will be his
world and
the world
at large.

(Confucius)

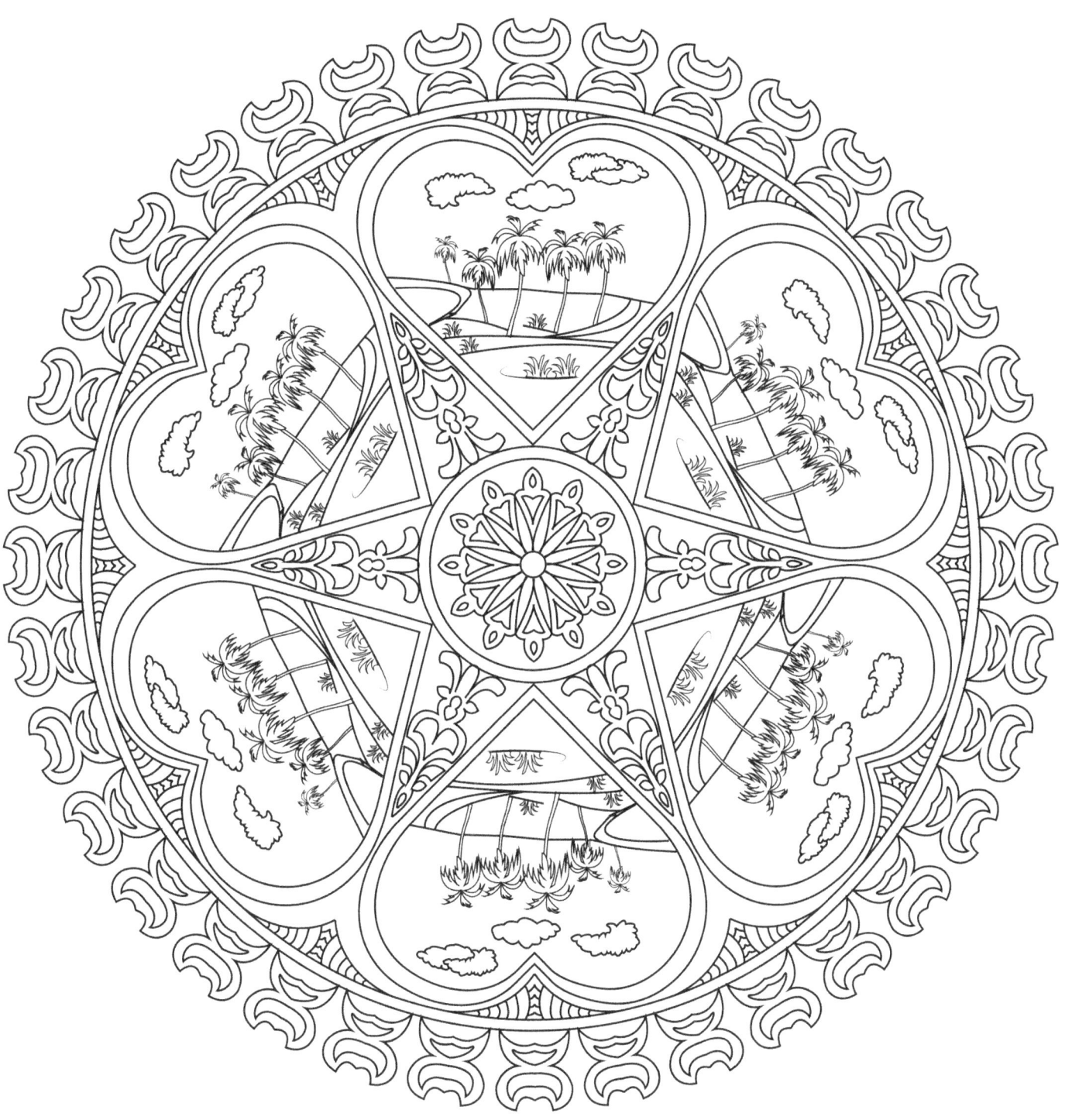

The
flowering
of love is
meditation.

(Jiddu Krishnamurti)

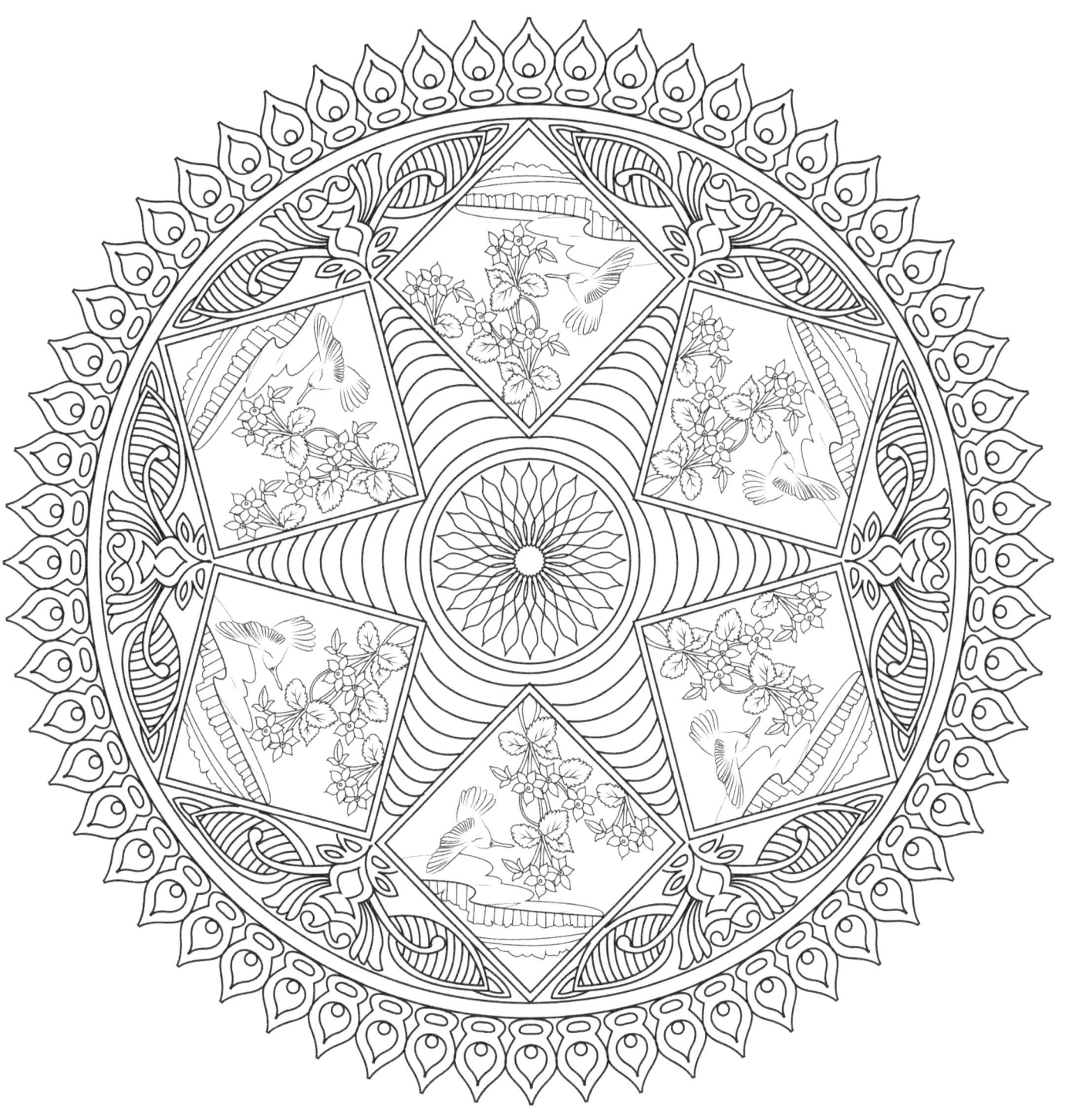

What you
do today
can improve
all your
tomorrows.

(Ralph Marston)